CADENCE

A COMPENDIUM OF ENGLISH LITERATURE

DR. ARUP RATAN BASAK AND SUJOY KUMAR ACHARJYA

To the ambitious young individuals endeavoring to create a brighter future, may this book illuminate your journey.

Contents

Preface

Preface

According to the new NEP rules established by the Central Board, a revised syllabus has been introduced for university and college students. In light of this change, there has been a noticeable lack of a comprehensive resource tailored to the specific needs of these students. Therefore, we are pleased to present a book that encompasses both the essential text and a variety of questions formatted in accordance with the semester examination syllabus. The included texts serve as preliminary readings and are complemented by thorough supplementary notes. It is important to note that answers to exam questions should be both concise and complete, addressing the specific needs of students preparing for their assessments. We express our gratitude to our loved ones, teachers, and colleagues for their encouragement and support in undertaking this endeavor.

Astrophil and Stella 1: Loving in truth, and fain in verse my love to show

Astrophil and Stella 1: Loving in truth, and fain in verse my love to show
BY SIR PHILIP SIDNEY

Loving in truth, and fain in verse my love to show,
That she, dear she, might take some pleasure of my pain,—
Pleasure might cause her read, reading might make her know,
Knowledge might pity win, and pity grace obtain,—
I sought fit words to paint the blackest face of woe;
Studying inventions fine her wits to entertain,
Oft turning others' leaves, to see if thence would flow
Some fresh and fruitful showers upon my sunburn'd brain.
But words came halting forth, wanting invention's stay;
Invention, Nature's child, fled step-dame Study's blows;

And others' feet still seem'd but strangers in my way.
Thus great with child to speak and helpless in my
throes,
Biting my truant pen, beating myself for spite,
"Fool," said my Muse to me, "look in thy heart, and
write."

Annotations:

Fain: with pleasure or willingly; **verse:** writing that is arranged in lines, often with regular rhythm or pattern of rhythm, here, poem; **Grace:** a quality of behavior that is polite and pleasant and deserve respect; **Fit words:** appropriate words; **Blackest face of woe:** the most horrible picture of sorrow; **Inventions:** the poems which are the poetic invention of other poets; **Wits:** intelligence; **Entertain:** to interest and amuse somebody in order to please them; **Thence:** from there; **Fresh and fruitful shower:** showers of inspiration, here compared to falling of rain on sunburnt parched land; **Halting:** to stop; **Step-dame:** step mother; **Feet:** the metrical feet of a poem, as well as the physical feet of other poets; **Great with child:** pregnant with poem inside; **Throes:** violent pain, especially at the moment of death, here during giving birth; **Truant:** disobedient; **Spite:** a feeling of wanting to hurt or upset somebody; **Muse:** Muse (in ancient Greek and Roman Stories) one of the nine goddesses who encouraged poetry, music and other branches of art and literature.

About the poem:

Astrophel and Stella is a sonnet sequence of 108 sonnets and 11 songs by Sir Philip Sydney. Some key points about this work include:

- Composed in the 1580s and published posthumously in 1591

- Considered one of the greatest sonnet sequences in English literature
- Tells the story of Stella ("star"), beloved by Astrophel ("star lover")
- Details passionate feelings, conflicting emotions, and the speaker's ultimate decision to abandon pursuit of Stella for public service
- Observes poetic conventions of reason and passion, wit and will
- Generated a vogue for sonnet sequences and influenced poets like Edmund Spenser.

About the Poet and his Age: Philip Sidney was a key figure in the Elizabethan age and a prominent writer of courtly love poetry. His sonnet sequence "Astrophel and Stella" is a prime example of this genre, and it is believed to have been inspired by his love for Penelope Devereux, the wife of Robert Rich, 1st Earl of Warwick .

Some characteristics of courtly love poetry include:
- Love for a lady who is often unavailable or unattainable
- Adoration and worship of the lady from afar
- Emphasis on the beauty and virtue of the lady
- Suffering and longing on the part of the lover
- Use of metaphor and other poetic devices to express the intensity of the lover's feelings

Sidney's poetry also shows the influence of Petrarchan sonnet conventions, which were popular during the Renaissance. His poetry is known for its lyricism, musicality, and clever use of language.

Courtly Love : Courtly love was a literary and philosophical movement that emerged in medieval Europe, particularly in the 12th and 13th centuries. It emphasized the adoration and worship of a lady from afar, often without expectation of physical gratification or reciprocation.

Key aspects of courtly love include:

1. Chivalrous devotion: The lover (usually a knight) devotes himself to the service of his lady, often without hope of reward.

2. Unattainability: The lady is often married, unavailable, or unattainable, making the love impossible.

3. Adoration from afar: The lover worships the lady from a distance, often without direct interaction.

4. Emphasis on virtue: The lady is idealized for her beauty, grace, and virtue.

5. Suffering and longing: The lover suffers from the pangs of love, often expressing his emotions through poetry, music, or other art forms.

6. Platonic idealism: Courtly love emphasizes the spiritual and intellectual aspects of love, rather than physical desire.

Courtly love was a cultural phenomenon that influenced literature, art, and music, shaping the way people thought about love and relationships. It continues to inspire artistic expression and influence modern conceptions of romantic love.

Contribution:

Sidney was the chief of an elegant coterie and exercised an influence which was almost supreme during his short life. He was the most commanding literary figure before the time of Spenser and Shakespeare. Like the best of Elizabethans, Sidney was successful in more than one branch of literature, but one of his works was published until after his death. His finest achievement in poetry was *Astrophel and Stella,* a collection of 108 love sonnets. This work saw the light of day in 1591. It is a collection of songs and sonnets, evidently addressed to one person. Lady Penelope Devereux, afterwards Lady Rich Sidney and Lady

Penelope had been betrothed when the latter was a child. For some reason the match was broken off and Lady Penelope married Lord Rich, with whom she lived for a while most unhappily. The sonnets written by Sidney owe much to Petrarch and Ronsard in tone and style. They reveal a true lyric emotion couched in a language delicately archaic. Sidney is undoubtedly the greatest literary figure between Wyatt and Spenser.

Line By Line Explanation of the sonnet Loving in Truth

Explanation of Lines 1 - 4:
"Loving in truth, and fain in verse my love to show,
That, She, dear She, might take some pleasure of my pain,
Pleasure might cause her read, reading might make her know;
Knowledge might pity win, and pity grace obtain"

"Loving in truth" means loving sincerely or whole heartedly. The poet in the person of a lover desires to express his love and sincere devotion in verse. "Knowledge" referred to here is how much the poet loves sincerely his lady-love. He is eager to show his sincere love for his lady-love in his verse because he thinks that if his beloved reads his verse, she may be pleased to know the poet's deep agony due to unfulfilled love and this knowledge may bring her pity to the poet. The lover here proposes to achieve her beloved's pity and grace by writing verse in her praise and spares no pain for the purpose.

Explanation of Lines 5 - 8:
"I sought fit words to paint the blackest face of woe,
Studying inventions fine, her wits to entertain,
Oft turning others' leaves, to see if thence would flow

Some fresh and fruitful showers upon my sunburnt brain."
In the sonnet "Loving in Truth", Sir Philip Sidney in the person of a lover expresses his desire to show his beloved his love in his verse written in her praise. He hopes that his effort, if successful may win ultimately for him her 'pity' and 'grace'. In his frantic effort to find 'fit words' to paint his deep pang caused by unfulfilled love, he attempts to find inspiration and guidance from other poets' works. Hence, he has often turned others' leaves that is the pages of books written by other poets.

The poet-lover here expresses his benumbed condition due to his unrequited love through the quoted lines. The poet-lover suffers from so much agony and pang of his unfulfilled love that his brain becomes completely unproductive. It has become dry and scorched like the heat-oppressed land of summer. So he seeks earnestly the showers of fresh thought and imagination of other poets upon his benumbed brain, so that it can produce appropriate verse to express his genuine love to his beloved.

Explanation of Lines 9 - 11:
"But words came halting forth, wanting Invention's stay;
Nature's child, fled step-dame Study's blows;
And others' feet still seemed but strangers in my way."
In the sonnet, "Loving in Truth", the poet-lover proposes to achieve his lady-love's pity and grace by writing verse in her praise. So he tries to imitate others' works but he fails. He realises that poetic fancy or imagination is a spontaneous expression and can not be imposed by imitation or guidance from others. So he realises that "Invention" is "Nature's Child".

The poet-lover here compares poetic imagination to a child and study to its step-mother. He compares so because true poetic imagination comes naturally and spontaneously, not by studying or borrowing others' imagination. Just as a child always tries to escape the clutch of its step-mother, similarly when the poet-lover, being unable to produce appropriate words to express his genuine love to his beloved, tries to take help of the words of others poets, those imagination borrowed from other poets try to escape and can not produce appropriate verse. Poetic invention evades the authority of the 'study' just as a child runs away from the command of his stepmother.

Explanation of Lines 12 - 14:

"Thus, great with child to speak, and helpless in my throes,
Biting my truant pen, beating myself for spite
Fool said my Muse to me look in thy heart, and write."

The quoted lines taken from Sir Philip Sidney's sonnet "Loving in Truth" from his sonnet-sequence "Astrophel and Stella" bring out the poet-lover's great agony for his inability to express his love to his beloved in appropriate words. In order to please her beloved by writing verse in her praise, the poet-lover indulges in frantic effort of finding 'fit words' for his expression. But he fails. So he feels 'helpless' and was in pain for he can not express his poetic urge in proper words. So, Sidney is called 'Fool' by the Muse (the inspirers of poetry) for his unfruitful effort. Just as a child not issued in time from its mother's womb causes pain of its mother, similarly the poet-lover

Questions Answers From The Sonnet Loving In Truth

1. Why does the poet-lover want to express his genuine love to his beloved?

Ans: In Sur Philip Sidney's sonnet "Loving in Truth" taken from his sonnet-sequence "Astrophel and Stella", the poet-lover wants to express his genuine love to his beloved in appropriate words through his verse because he thinks that if his beloved reads his verse, she may be pleased to know the poet's deep agony due to unfulfilled love and this knowledge may bring her pity and grace to the poet.

2. How does the poet try to win the lady-love's pity and grace?

Ans: The poet-lover in Sir Philip Sidney's sonnet "Loving in Truth" tries desperately to express his genuine love to his beloved in appropriate words of his verse. But as he is unable to create appropriate words, he reads extensively the fine imagination and feelings expressed in others' verses and tries to imitate the works of others. But he absolutely fails in his efforts.

3. What type of sonnet is Loving in Truth?

Ans: Sir Philip Sidney's sonnet "Loving in Truth" is cast in the mould of a typical Petrarchan sonnet of 14 lines and is divisible into the octave and sestet. While the octave presents the efforts of the poet at writing poetry, the sestet narrates his failure and subsequent realization.

4. Is the sonnet "Loving in Truth" a lamentation of a lover?

Ans: In "Loving in Truth" we find a lover who tries to express his sincere love and thus to gain mastery in his literary talent. But he does not appear as a lover who violently laments over his rejection of love. He is free from any angry denunciation and distraction. His love is absolute and unconditional. He remains satisfied in expressing his love through his verse. Lover here emerges as a follower of selfless ideal to be sought sincerely.

5. Why there is reference of "Muse" in the sonnet "Loving in Truth"?

Ans: According to classical mythology, Muses are said to be nine goddesses who inspire poetry, music, painting etc. Here in the sonnet, 'Muse' stands for poetic inspiration which according the realisation of Sidney, comes from the core of the heart. This invocation also confirms to the Elizabethan poetic tradition and it is also an example of Sidney's wit and humour.

6. In what way "Loving in Truth" is a typical reflection of the poetic feeling of the times?

Ans: All the sonnets of the period reveal the same spirit of passion and regret highlighted by the poet whose poems are characterised by a similar Elizabethan tone of eternalizing his lover through emotion displayed through poetry.

Short questions and answers from Loving in Truth.

1) "In verse my love to show"- Why does the poet want to write verse? How does the poet want to show his love in verse?

Ans:- Sidney was disappointed in love. The poet's love was true and he was particularly keen to show it in his verse written in praise of his lady-love. He wanted to put his suffering in his verse so that his lady- love might be pleased at his efforts and learn of his suffering. Her knowledge of love might make her pitiful to him. Her pity might lead her to show her favour to the poet. The poet expects to win her grace by means of his verse written in her praise.

The poet wants to show the pangs of his love-lorn heart by painting his innermost afflictions and woes in lucid rhymes. He wants to sketch a lurid picture of his agony in words. He would portray them in the deepest dye of injured feelings that may stir the depths of his lady love's compassion and draw her attention to him.

2) **"Biting my truant pen...." - Where does this line occur? What is meant by truant pen? Why did the poet bite his pen?**

Ans:- The line occurs in the poem 'Loving in Truth' written by Philip Sidney.

'Truant pen' means which go astray and does not obey the heart like a naughty school boy who runs away from his school. Here Sidney refers to his inability to express himself.

The poet bites his pen to indicate the state of his mental restlessness. He grows angry with himself for his failure to express his poetic feeling. It is well suggestive of a lover's psychology and his utter helplessness caused by intense passion of love.

3) **"Fool said my Muse to me..."- Where does this line occur? Who was the Muse? What did the Muse say?**

Ans:- The line occurs in "Loving in Truth" by Philip Sidney.

The 'Muse' according to classical tradition is the goddess of learning. She is the guiding poetic spirit, the inspirer of poetry.

The Muse's advice to Sidney to look into his heart for words indicates the triumph of the inspirational theory of poetry. Poetry is born out of inspiration. It is not a product imitation. Its spontaneous and natural source is the human heart, the receptacle of all emotions, feelings and thoughts. So, the poet should delve deep into his heart instead of looking here and there for his poetic inspiration.

Critical Commentary

The first I the sequence of songs and sonnets, *Astrophel and stella* was printed three times in quarto in 1591, and revised and rearranged from a better text by Sideny's sister, the Countess of Pembroke, in the folio edition of Sidney's Arcadia and other works,1598.The Astrophel in title means 'star-lover' and is the popet himself while Stella is the 'star' or Penelope Devereux.

One of the central concepts or themes of the poem is the question of the source of creativity. Where does creativity come from? A question which has found few answers and as Plato commented, it may be ascribed to a sort of religious exultation with great revolutionary frenzy. Yet when the muse is non-condescending the poet is left a common man unable to find fit words for his poetry. An answer to the question can be found in Sidney's poem and can be considered to be its central theme.

The first poem in the sonnet sequence, their names tell us the story of their relationship. "Astro" is from the Greek for "star", while "Phel"or "Phil" means love, so he is literally "starvlover". He orbits round and round the radiant Stella, whose name is derived from the Latin for star. Thus, together, the poet and his beloved express the Greco-Roman harmony of feeling and form, a classical sensibility revived during the Renaissance.

In the first four lines of the poem, we find Astrophel setting forth his artistic manifesto – he would 'fain' or want/desire/aspire to put his love into verse, because the agony of his secret passion might then be transmuted into something attractive. Its beauty might make her read and from the reading would develop an understanding of his plight. Such understanding might then win her pity, and finally her grace.

Then the poet sets about preparing for his composition and his initial thought is to copy from the poems of masters but as hard as he might try, the spark does not come. The words that do come 'want' or lack 'invention's stay'. Invention which we can read as the faculty of the imagination , is the child of Nature. It relies on a mind that freely responds to the world as it unfolds in the present. It flees from book-bound studies – here personified as false parent, the archetypal bullying step mother. At the same time he was also intimidated by the works of the ancient ports and to underscore this, Sidney puns on 'feet' , with the double meaning of metrical feet. At such a point when he is about to give up and chews his disobedient pen, the muse arrives and informs him that he has been foolish enough and from now on should concentrate on his own heart and find his inspiration for his own feelings of woe and sorrow.

The poem was most probably composed in the 1580s and the sonnet sequence consists of 108 sonnets and 11 songs. The sequence was a watershed inEnglish Renaissance poetry, in which Sidney partly nativized the key features of his Italian model Petrarch. These include an ongoing but partly obscure narrative ; the philosophical trappings of the poet in relation to love and desire; the musings on the art of poetic creation.

Loving in Truth by Sir Philip Sidney as a love poem.....

Sir Philip Sidney, as a poet, is found opposed to all poetic conventions and affectations even when he adheres to the primary forms and generic qualities of contemporary English poetry. However, his sonnets are free from the artificiality of conventional poetic works and are distinctly sincere. As seen in his sonnet "Loving in Truth", certain traits of his personality emerge significantly. It is the first poem in his sequence, "Astrophel and Stella" and seems to contain the bearings of his lover's pulse, in suspense and expectation.

Along with frank subjectivity and intense sincerity, "Loving in Truth" is enriched with rich imagination, a characteristic gift of the renaissance. Thematically, the poem is an open admission of the poet's futile efforts to please his beloved through verse offerings. The poem signifies how he fails to find inspiration for his poetic composition from serious study and laborious imitation. His eagerness to draw her attention and thereby to win her favour thus fails till he realizes that true inspiration lies at the core of his heart. The central theme of the sonnet lies in the concluding couplet in which the poet identifies the true source of inspiration in spontaneity of expression: "Look in thy heart and write."

Indeed, the poem rings with a lover's intimate feelings and sufferings. Love is seen as an ideal that requires selfless dedication and earnest yearning. Sidney's tone is animated with an idealistic zeal, which is free from egoism. The singleness of emotion, pertaining to love, that characterized the Petrarchan sonnet is also found in this poem. There is, no doubt, a transition in the poet's mood from the octave to the sestet, but the essential unity is always present and the emotional content remains unaltered.

The sonnet is rich in imagery that is pleasant but precise. The analogies of "other's leaves" and "fresh and fruitful showers" are well conceived, and the metaphor of "sun-burned brain" is very original. Equally interesting are his personifications of "Invention", "Nature" and "Study". There is usually no vagueness about his images. Even farfetched expressions like "Step- dame study's blows" and "truant pen" are quite witty and relevant to his contention.

The poem is not a helpless lament of a lover. It has no angry declination or renunciation, but rather filled with amorous optimism. There is hardly any monotonous glorification of unrequited love. However, structurally, the poem is Petrarchan in its division of theme into eight and six lines. There are some variations in the metrical arrangement and the lines are found to rhyme alternately, except the concluding couplet. The octave (the first eight lines) consists of the poet's frantic efforts to please his beloved by his poetry. The sestet (remaining six lines) shows his failure and final realization. His diction is well chosen while his imagery is plain yet impressive.

The poem, therefore, both conforms to and deviates from the contemporary style of sonnet writing. It is characterized by a blend of wit and sensibility, of intellectual brilliance and temperamental ardor. Sidney's sonnets, in their directness and spontaneity, remain an intimate record of the mind of a man who was both sincere and chivalrous. In his depth of sincerity and range of subjectivity, Sidney remains no less great than Shakespeare himself. His poems represent one of the most genial and original literary expressions of a true poet's profound emotion of love.

****

CHAPTER TWO

To His Coy Mistress

To His Coy Mistress
BY ANDREW MARVELL
Had we but world enough and time,
This coyness, lady, were no crime.
We would sit down, and think which way
To walk, and pass our long love's day.
Thou by the Indian Ganges' side
Shouldst rubies find; I by the tide
Of Humber would complain. I would
Love you ten years before the flood,
And you should, if you please, refuse
Till the conversion of the Jews.
My vegetable love should grow
Vaster than empires and more slow;
An hundred years should go to praise
Thine eyes, and on thy forehead gaze;
Two hundred to adore each breast,
But thirty thousand to the rest;
An age at least to every part,
And the last age should show your heart.
For, lady, you deserve this state,
Nor would I love at lower rate.
But at my back I always hear

Time's wingèd chariot hurrying near;
And yonder all before us lie
Deserts of vast eternity.
Thy beauty shall no more be found;
Nor, in thy marble vault, shall sound
My echoing song; then worms shall try
That long-preserved virginity,
And your quaint honour turn to dust,
And into ashes all my lust;
The grave's a fine and private place,
But none, I think, do there embrace.
Now therefore, while the youthful hue
Sits on thy skin like morning dew,
And while thy willing soul transpires
At every pore with instant fires,
Now let us sport us while we may,
And now, like amorous birds of prey,
Rather at once our time devour
Than languish in his slow-chapped power.
Let us roll all our strength and all
Our sweetness up into one ball,
And tear our pleasures with rough strife
Through the iron gates of life:
Thus, though we cannot make our sun
Stand still, yet we will make him run.

About the poet:

Andrew Marvell (born March 31, 1621, Winestead, Yorkshire, England—died August 18, 1678, London) was an English poet whose political reputation overshadowed that of his poetry until the 20th century. He is now considered to be one of the best Metaphysical poets.

Marvell was educated at Hull grammar school and Trinity College, Cambridge, taking a B.A. in 1639. His father's death in 1641 may have ended Marvell's promising academic career. He was abroad for at least five years (1642–46), presumably as a tutor. In 1651–52 he was tutor to Mary, daughter of Lord Fairfax, the Parliamentary general, at Nun Appleton, Yorkshire, during which time he probably wrote his notable poems "Upon Appleton House" and "The Garden" as well as his series of Mower poems.

Although earlier opposed to Oliver Cromwell'sCommonwealth government, he wrote "An Horatian Ode upon Cromwell's Return from Ireland" (1650), and from 1653 to 1657 he was a tutor to Cromwell's ward William Dutton. In 1657 he became assistant to John Milton as Latin secretary in the foreign office. "The First Anniversary" (1655) and "On the Death of O.C." (1659) showed his continued and growing admiration for Cromwell. In 1659 he was elected member of Parliament for Hull, an office he held until his death, serving skillfully and effectively.

After the restoration of Charles II in 1660, Marvell turned to political verse satires—the most notable was *The Last Instructions to a Painter*, against Lord Clarendon, Charles's lord chancellor—and prose political satire, notably *The Rehearsal Transpros'd* (1672–73). Marvell is also said to have interceded on behalf of Milton to have him freed from prison in 1660. He wrote a commendatory poem for the second edition of Milton's *Paradise Lost*. His political writings favoured the toleration of religious dissent and attacked the abuse of monarchical power.

At Marvell's death, his housekeeper-servant Mary Palmer claimed to be his widow, although this was undoubtedly a legal fiction. The first publication of his poems in 1681 resulted from a manuscript volume she found among his effects.

While Marvell's political reputation has faded and his reputation as a satirist is on a par with others of his time, his small body of lyric poems, first recommended in the 19th century by Charles Lamb, has since appealed to many readers, and in the 20th century he came to be considered one of the most notable poets of his century. Marvell was eclectic: his "To His Coy Mistress" is a classic of Metaphysical poetry; the Cromwell odes are the work of a classicist; his attitudes are sometimes those of the elegant Cavalier poets; and his nature poems resemble those of the Puritan Platonists. In "To His Coy Mistress," which is one of the most famous poems in the English language, the impatient poet urges his mistress to abandon her false modesty and submit to his embraces before time and death rob them of the opportunity to love.

Theme of Love and Death in the poem:

"To His Coy Mistress" is a love poem: it celebrates beauty, youth, and sexual pleasure. However, the speaker of the poem is haunted by mortality. Though he imagines a luxuriously slow love that takes thousands of years to reach consummation, he knows such a thing is impossible: he will die before it can be accomplished. Death cannot be delayed or defeated; the only response to death, according to the speaker, is to enjoy as much pleasure as possible before it comes. He urges the woman he loves not to wait, to enjoy the pleasures of life without restraint. The poem draws a contrast between two kinds of love: the full, rich love that would be possible if everyone lived forever, and the rushed, panicked love that mortal beings are forced to enjoy.

The first stanza of the poem poses a question and explores a hypothetical world: what would love be like if humans had infinite time to love? In response, the speaker imagines a world of unlimited pleasure. For example, he describes his mistress finding precious stones on the banks of the Ganges; he describes himself spending two hundred years praising a single part of her body.

The key to this paradise, then, is that the normal limitations of human life have been removed. The sheer length of the mistress's and the speaker's lives allows them to delay consummation of their love indefinitely: the speaker announces that his mistress might "refuse / 'Till the conversion of the Jews"—which, in the Christian theology of Marvell's time, was expected to occur during the biblical Last Days. In this ideal world, the speaker feels no urgency to consummate their relationship.

The speaker has no questions about whether his mistress deserves this long courtship, but he does have qualms about its viability. He is, he notes at the start of stanza 2, always conscious of the passage of time—and thus of the fact that both he and his mistress will eventually die. Stanza 2 diverges from the beautiful dream of stanza 1, reflecting instead on the pressing, inescapable threat of death.

Death, as the speaker imagines it, is the opposite of the paradise presented in stanza 1: instead of endless pleasure, it offers "deserts of vast eternity." The speaker's view of death is secular; he is not afraid of going to Hell or being punished for his sins. Instead, he fears death because it cuts short his and his mistress's capacity to enjoy each other. In death, he complains, her beauty will be lost and—unless she consents to have sex before she dies—her virginity will be taken by worms. The language of this stanza is grotesque. This is a poem of seduction, but it feels profoundly unsexy. The speaker's horror of death overshadows his erotic passion, but it also makes the speaker seem more sincere: while at first it might seem that the speaker is saying all these things primarily because he just wants to have some sex, the despair in the poem implies that the speaker's arguments are not mere rhetorical statements but rather deeply held beliefs and fears.

In the final stanza of the poem, the speaker finally announces his core argument: since death is coming—and since it will strip away the pleasures of the flesh—his mistress should agree to have sex with him soon. What's more, he imagines that their erotic "sport" will offer compensation for the pain and suffering of life. "Our pleasures," he argues, will tear through "the iron gates of life." Though he does not imagine that their pleasure will defeat death, he does believe that pleasure is the only reasonable response to death. Indeed, he even says that enjoying pleasure is a way to defy death. However, the grotesque language of stanza 2 may overwhelm the poem's insistence on the power of pleasure. If sexuality is a way to contest the power of death, it nonetheless seems—even in the speaker's own estimation—that death is an overwhelming, irresistible force.

Summary:

The speaker of "To His Coy Mistress" is an anonymous male lover who desires to have sex with his mistress. It is clear from his sustained attempt to seduce this anonymous woman that the speaker is motivated primarily by sexual arousal. For example, though he speaks generally of his love for his mistress, he also makes fairly explicit reference to his erect genitalia when he tells her, "My vegetable love should grow / Vaster than empires" (lines 11–12). The speaker then spends the next six lines looking over his mistress's body, naming the various parts of her that he would like to "praise." Finally, as the poem nears its conclusion, the speaker fantasizes about the strenuous physicality of lovemaking. He tells his mistress, "Let us roll all our strength and all / Our sweetness up into one ball, / And tear our pleasures with rough strife" (lines 41–43). The lengths this speaker goes to convince his reluctant mistress to have sex with him make it clear just how *excited* he is.

And yet, despite his evident arousal, the desire for sex may not be the speaker's only motivation. Instead, his insistence on the need to seize the moment may well reflect an existential crisis related to his own mortality. In the poem's second stanza, the speaker moves away from his fantasy of infinite time and space and turns to images of aging and death. He invites his mistress to imagine the fading of her own beauty, then he conjures a vision of worms eating her corpse. On the one hand, the speaker is using these images to shock his mistress, believing that her own fear of decline will convince her to make love. On the other hand, there is also the hint of something more personal in the way the speaker introduces the subjects of aging and death. He says: "But at my back I always hear / Time's wingèd chariot hurrying near" (lines 21–22). Instead of making a more general claim about the passage of time, the speaker specifically refers to his own experience here, suggesting that he may have a personal preoccupation with his own eventual death. In this case, his motivation may stem as much from a desire for sex as from a fear of his own mortality.

Marvell is an impressive stalwart in the metaphysical tradition not just for his copious use of characteristically metaphysical wit, conceits and imageries, his exhibition of pointed erudition, and strangeness in expression that affects one's intellect as much as his emotion, but also for the argumentative and logical evolution of his lyrics that shows a peculiar blend of passion and thought. This trait is the most visible in *To His Coy Mistress*. The poem is itself an argument and presses itself towards a conclusion by seemingly logical steps. The subject and structure of the poem is conceived of and expressed by Marvell syllogistically. The logical structure of the poem is best understood from the manner in which the three stanzas open.

> "Had we but World enough, and Time,
> This coyness Lady were no crime....
> But at my back I always hear
> Times winged Charriot hurrying near.....
> Now therefore......
> .....let us sport us while we may...."

The dialectic of the poem does not only reign supreme in the formal demonstration which is so explicit in the three strophes of the poem, the three strophes that have a syllogistic relation to one another, but also in the apparent contrasts evoked by the imageries they include. Recognizably the theme of the poem is of the great traditional commonplaces of European literature, as it is evident, as the poem opens with a battery of hyperboles, all meant to praise the lady, or the anatomy of this lady.

The opening sentence of the poem:

"Had we but World enough and Time...."

The 'Had' helps the poet create to make –believe situation or condition which is actually the incipient, suppositious proposition, the first premise of his argument. The 'Had' allows him to state explicitly a condition which is very much contrary to fact. The 'Had' also enables him to grammatically establish his assertion that 'we' do not have 'World enough and Time'. What follows this is a series of imageries, conceits and a subtle display of wit to build the make-believe state of love experience. He says that (if they had endless space and time) the bashful attitude of the poet's mistress would not have been a transgression or felony. In such an impossible case they would spend away their time deciding on the path they would take and then idly squander lavishly their endless time of love. Marvell intensifies the impossibility of the situation by means of two hyperboles; the first stretching the spatial limits, and the second expanding the temporal boundary.

"Thou by the Indian Ganges side

Should'st Rubies find: I by the tide

Of Humber would complain"

Thus, the poet sends the two lovers to the diametrically opposite ends of the equator – the East and the West. Marvell, simultaneously, makes his instrument the contemporary (mis)conception which was so popular among gentry in the Elizabethan era with regards to the esoteric east. Thus while the lady would spend time seeking for rubies in the Ganges, the lover himself would grumble at his lady's coyness and indifference to carnal love by the tide of Humber. The vastness or infinitude of both time and space is again ingeniously verbalized in his witty reference to two Biblical allusions; the 'Flood' mentioned in the Old Testament and the conversion of the Jews to devout Christians just before the end of the world.

"......I would

Love you ten years before the Flood:

And you should if you please refuse

Till the conversion of the Jews."

The first premise attains a climactic point with the poet's use of metaphysical conceits :

"My vegetable Love should grow

Vaster than empires, and more slow."

The 'vegetable Love' can easily be explained if one keeps in mind the tradition in which Marvell is writing. In the metaphysical tradition the poets discovered propositions referring to one field of experience in terms of an intellectual structure derived from another field, and often from the field of great erudition. The 'vegetable Love' is a curious attribution to love. The idea of the ceaseless growth of love alone is implied. The growth of love is like the growth of plants or trees and therefore slow and steady. In short the first stanza begins with a suppositious proposition, and the rest of it offers a series of hooks upon which Marvell hangs his hyperboles, conceits and wit to compliment the premise.

The indispensable 'But' with which the second stanza opens is just too sufficient not to disown the make-believe condition the first stanza build. The second stanza shows the element of urgency and crescendo in the poet's use of words. It shows the immediate necessity to reject the suppositious proposition. The poet delineates a poetic picture of the relentless reality by another series of counter-imagery and counter-wit. The image of the 'winged Charriot', forms a sort of fulcrum on which the poem turns, and the love theme becomes a semi-shadowy illustration of the effect which time has upon human life. The poet's obsession with the idea of the inevitable and terrible onrush of time balances the former, impossible idea of his fantastic imagination of endless courtship. Contrary to his 'vegetable love' he now visualizes 'Deserts of vast Eternity'. Running counter to his earlier desire to admire the anatomical details of his mistress for seemingly endless ages, he now writes,

"Thy beauty shall no more be found;
Nor, in thy marble vault, shall sound

My echoing song; then worms shall try
That long-preserved virginity,
And your quaint honour turn to dust,
And into ashes all my lust;

But though the poet has quiet substantiated his argument, the cause for his denial of the first premise, he does not cease then and there. Before stating on the consequence of his rejecting the supposed proposition he writes,

"The grave's a fine and private place,
But none, I think, do there embrace."

The apparent erotic suggestion mingles inseparably with the subtle element of irony in these lines to show the ironical state that their love and lust might reach because of the lady's abstaining from all carnal intemperance.

Thus, being compelled by normal human experience and his urgent recognition of reality, the poet comes, finally, to the logical conclusion when the poet says,

" Now therefore, while the youthful hue
Sits on thy skin like morning dew,
And while thy willing soul transpires
At every pore with instant fires,
Now let us sport us while we may,
And now, like amorous birds of prey,
Rather at once our time devour
Than languish in his slow-chapped power.
Let us roll all our strength and all
Our sweetness up into one ball,
And tear our pleasures with rough strife
Through the iron gates of life:"

The *carpe diem* (snatch the day) motif, which can be assessed as the motto of epicureanism, becomes a luminescent idea towards the end as the poet says,

"Thus, though we cannot make our sun
Stand still, yet we will make him run."

In brief, the general structure of the poem *To His Coy Mistress* is syllogistic, but the poetic quality involves several non-syllogistic elements as well.

Metaphysical Poetry:

Metaphysical poetry is a group of poems that share common characteristics: they are all highly intellectualized, use rather strange imagery, use frequent paradox and contain extremely complicated thought. Literary critic and poet Samuel Johnson first coined the term 'metaphysical poetry' in his book Lives of the Most Eminent English Poets (1179-1781). In the book, Johnson wrote about a group of 17th-century British poets that included John Donne, George Herbert, Richard Crashaw, Andrew Marvell and Henry Vaughan. He noted how the poets shared many common characteristics, especially ones of wit and elaborate style.

What Does Metaphysical Mean?

The word 'meta' means 'after,' so the literal translation of 'metaphysical' is 'after the physical.' Basically, metaphysics deals with questions that can't be explained by science. It questions the nature of reality in a philosophical way. • Here are some common metaphysical questions: • Does God exist? • Is there a difference between the way things appear to us and the way they really are? Essentially, what is the difference between reality and perception? • Is everything that happens already predetermined? If so, then is free choice non-existent? • Is consciousness limited to the brain? Metaphysics can cover a broad range of topics from religious to consciousness; however, all the questions about metaphysics ponder the nature of reality. And of course, there is no one correct answer to any of these questions. Metaphysics is about exploration and philosophy, not about science and math.

DEVICES USED IN METAPHYSICAL POETRY:

Metaphysical poets like John Donne use complex, dramatic expressions and a variety of literary devices like extended conceits, paradoxes, and imagery in colloquial and personal language that challenges ideas of morality, traditional love, and carnality; it is intellectually inventive even jarring sometimes because it mixes and links two unlike things to create extended metaphors and anecdotes that is unique in comparison to previous poets of his era particularly Edmund Spenser.

Metaphysical conceits are of Central importance in metaphysical poetry. A (metaphysical) conceit is usually classified as a subtype of metaphor – an elaborate and strikingly unconventional or supposedly far-fetched metaphor, hyperbole, contradiction, simile, paradox or oxymoron causing a shock to the reader by the obvious dissimilarity, "distance" between or stunning incompatibility of the objects compared. One of the most famous conceits is John Donne's A Valediction: Forbidding Mourning, a poem in which Donne compares two souls in love to the points on a geometer's compass

CHARACTERISTICS OF METAPHYSICAL POETRY?

• The group of metaphysical poets that we mentioned earlier is obviously not the only poets or philosophers or writers that deal with metaphysical questions. There are other more specific characteristics that prompted Johnson to place the 17th-century poets together.

• Perhaps the most common characteristic is that metaphysical poetry contained large doses of wit. In fact, although the poets were examining serious questions about the existence of God or whether a human could possibly perceive the world, the poets were sure to ponder those questions with humor.

• Metaphysical poetry also sought to shock the reader and wake him or her up from his or her normal existence in order to question the unquestionable. The poetry often mixed ordinary speech with paradoxes and puns. The results were strange, comparing unlikely things, such as lovers to a compass or the soul to a drop of dew. These weird comparisons were called conceits.

Metaphysical poetry also explored a few common themes. They all had a religious sentiment. In addition, many of the poems explored the theme of carpe diem (seize the day) and investigated the humanity of life. One great way to analyze metaphysical poetry is to consider how the poems are about both thought and feeling. Think about it. How could you possibly write a poem about the existence of God if you didn't have some emotional reaction to such an enormous, life altering question?

Metaphysical poetry investigates the relation between rational, logical argument on the one hand and intuition or "mysticism" on the other, often depicted with sensuous detail Metaphysical poetry is considered highly ambiguous due to high intellect and knowledge of metaphysical poets.

Short Questions and Answers

1. Who is the speaker in "To His Coy Mistress"?

Answer: The speaker is a passionate lover addressing his beloved, trying to persuade her to stop being coy.

2. What is the central theme of the poem?

Answer: The main theme is Carpe Diem—the idea that life is short, so one must seize the present moment.

3. What does "Had we but world enough, and time" mean?

Answer: It means that if they had unlimited time and space, her shyness would not be a problem.

4. How long does the speaker say he would love her if time were unlimited?

Answer: He says he would love her for ages—like spending hundreds and thousands of years to praise her beauty.

5. What image does the poet use to show the passing of time?

Answer: The image of "Time's wingèd chariot hurrying near."

6. What does the speaker warn will happen in the grave?

Answer: He warns that in the grave, her beauty will turn to dust and "worms shall try that long-preserved virginity."

7. What is the tone of the first section of the poem?

Answer: It is calm, romantic, and hyperbolic, showing ideal love.

8. What is the tone of the second section?

Answer: It becomes urgent and realistic, focusing on the brevity of life.

9. What does the speaker propose in the final section?

Answer: He proposes that they should embrace love passionately while they are still young.

10. What figure of speech is used in "Time's wingèd chariot"?

Answer: It is a metaphor and also contains personification, as time is imagined as a charioteer.

11. What does "vegetable love" mean in the poem?

Answer: It refers to a love that grows slowly and steadily, taking ages to mature.

12. Why does the speaker mention rivers like the Ganges and the Humber?

Answer: To show the distance between the lovers and stress idealized vs. real settings.

13. What is the rhyme scheme of "To His Coy Mistress"?

Answer: AA BB CC DD... (rhyming couplets in iambic tetrameter).

14. What type of poem is this?

Answer: It is a metaphysical poem with logical arguments and witty imagery.

15. What final argument does the poet use to persuade his mistress?

Answer: He argues that since they cannot stop time, they should make the most of the time they have by uniting in love.

Long Questions and Answers

1. Discuss "To His Coy Mistress" as a Carpe Diem poem.

Answer:

"To His Coy Mistress" is one of the finest examples of the Carpe Diem (seize the day) tradition in English poetry. Andrew Marvell structures the poem as a persuasive argument in which the speaker urges his beloved to overcome her coyness and embrace love while there is still time. The poem is divided into three logical sections: "If we had time," "But time is limited," and "Therefore let us act now."

In the first section, the speaker imagines a world in which time is infinite. He uses hyperbolic images—spending centuries admiring her eyes, breasts, and heart—to suggest that he would willingly wait forever if life were eternal. However, in the second section, the tone shifts dramatically as the poet introduces the reality of mortality through the metaphor "Time's wingèd chariot hurrying near." Death becomes an inevitable force that threatens youthful beauty and unfulfilled desire. The frightening images of the grave, dust, and worms emphasize the futility of delaying love.

Finally, in the third section, he argues that since time is short, they must "make the most" of the present moment. Their passionate union, he claims, can make time run faster but more meaningfully. Thus, the poem conveys the central idea of Carpe Diem: youth is fleeting, time is limited, and love must be embraced before it is too late.

2. Examine the poetic techniques used by Marvell in "To His Coy Mistress."

Answer:

Marvell employs a number of poetic devices characteristic of metaphysical poetry. The poem is written in rhyming couplets (heroic couplets) with regular iambic tetrameter, giving it a smooth, persuasive rhythm. His argument is highly logical, structured like a syllogism: "If we had time... But we don't... Therefore let us love now."

One of the key techniques is Marvell's use of hyperbole, especially in the first section. He exaggerates the time he would spend appreciating each part of her body, reflecting both admiration and playful wit. Metaphors and imagery add depth: "vegetable love" suggests slow organic growth, while "Time's wingèd chariot" personifies time as a threatening pursuer.

In the second section, the poet uses macabre imagery—the grave, dust, and worms—to create a sense of urgency. The final section shifts to vivid imagery of passion and intensity, comparing the lovers to birds of prey who "tear our pleasures with rough strife." This dramatic contrast enhances the persuasive logic of the poem. Marvell's combination of wit, argument, imagery, and rhythm makes the poem a powerful example of metaphysical style.

3. How does Marvell structure his argument in "To His Coy Mistress"?

Answer:

Marvell builds his argument through a clear three-part structure resembling a logical proof.

First Section (Hypothesis – If): The poet imagines an ideal world where time is abundant. He tells his mistress that if they had "world enough, and time," her coyness would not matter. This section is filled with lavish imagery, exaggerations, and dreams of eternal love.

Second Section (Reality – But): He then presents the harsh truth that time is limited. The tone becomes urgent, and he introduces the famous metaphor "Time's wingèd chariot hurrying near." He warns that death will soon claim both beauty and opportunity.

Third Section (Conclusion – Therefore): Finally, the speaker concludes that since time is short and life is uncertain, they should make use of the present moment. He proposes that their passionate love will give meaning to fleeting time.

This logical progression—from idealism to realism to urgency—strengthens the persuasive power of his argument and reflects the metaphysical poets' love of reasoning and wit.

4. Explain the role of imagery in "To His Coy Mistress."

Answer:

Imagery plays a crucial role in shaping the emotional and intellectual impact of the poem. In the first section, Marvell uses romantic and exaggerated imagery to show how endlessly he would adore his beloved if time were limitless. Phrases like "My vegetable love should grow / Vaster than empires" create a sense of expansion and eternity.

In the second section, the imagery becomes dark and frightening, emphasizing the brevity of life. The metaphor "Time's wingèd chariot" evokes a sense of relentless pursuit. Graveyard images—"deserts of vast eternity," "worms," and "dust"—contrast sharply with the earlier romanticism, highlighting the reality of mortality.

The final section shifts again to fiery and energetic imagery. Lovers become like birds of prey, devouring pleasure "with rough strife," symbolizing the intense vitality they must embrace. This combination of calm, dark, and passionate imagery helps Marvell make his central argument dramatically effective.

****

CHAPTER THREE

Lycidas

Lycidas
BY JOHN MILTON
Yet once more, O ye laurels, and once more
Ye myrtles brown, with ivy never sere,
I come to pluck your berries harsh and crude,
And with forc'd fingers rude
Shatter your leaves before the mellowing year.
Bitter constraint and sad occasion dear
Compels me to disturb your season due;
For Lycidas is dead, dead ere his prime,
Young Lycidas, and hath not left his peer.
Who would not sing for Lycidas? he knew
Himself to sing, and build the lofty rhyme.
He must not float upon his wat'ry bier
Unwept, and welter to the parching wind,
Without the meed of some melodious tear.
Begin then, Sisters of the sacred well
That from beneath the seat of Jove doth spring;
Begin, and somewhat loudly sweep the string.
Hence with denial vain and coy excuse!
So may some gentle muse
With lucky words favour my destin'd urn,
And as he passes turn

And bid fair peace be to my sable shroud!
For we were nurs'd upon the self-same hill,
Fed the same flock, by fountain, shade, and rill;
Together both, ere the high lawns appear'd
Under the opening eyelids of the morn,
We drove afield, and both together heard
What time the gray-fly winds her sultry horn,
Batt'ning our flocks with the fresh dews of night,
Oft till the star that rose at ev'ning bright
Toward heav'n's descent had slop'd his westering
wheel.
Meanwhile the rural ditties were not mute,
Temper'd to th'oaten flute;
Rough Satyrs danc'd, and Fauns with clov'n heel,
From the glad sound would not be absent long;
And old Damætas lov'd to hear our song.
But O the heavy change now thou art gone,
Now thou art gone, and never must return!
Thee, Shepherd, thee the woods and desert caves,
With wild thyme and the gadding vine o'ergrown,
And all their echoes mourn.
The willows and the hazel copses green
Shall now no more be seen
Fanning their joyous leaves to thy soft lays.
As killing as the canker to the rose,
Or taint-worm to the weanling herds that graze,
Or frost to flowers that their gay wardrobe wear
When first the white thorn blows:
Such, Lycidas, thy loss to shepherd's ear.
Where were ye, Nymphs, when the remorseless deep
Clos'd o'er the head of your lov'd Lycidas?
For neither were ye playing on the steep
Where your old bards, the famous Druids, lie,

Nor on the shaggy top of Mona high,
Nor yet where Deva spreads her wizard stream.
Ay me! I fondly dream
Had ye bin there'—for what could that have done?
What could the Muse herself that Orpheus bore,
The Muse herself, for her enchanting son,
Whom universal nature did lament,
When by the rout that made the hideous roar
His gory visage down the stream was sent,
Down the swift Hebrus to the Lesbian shore?
Alas! what boots it with incessant care
To tend the homely, slighted shepherd's trade,
And strictly meditate the thankless Muse?
Were it not better done, as others use,
To sport with Amaryllis in the shade,
Or with the tangles of Neæra's hair?
Fame is the spur that the clear spirit doth raise
(That last infirmity of noble mind)
To scorn delights and live laborious days;
But the fair guerdon when we hope to find,
And think to burst out into sudden blaze,
Comes the blind Fury with th'abhorred shears,
And slits the thin-spun life. "But not the praise,"
Phoebus replied, and touch'd my trembling ears;
"Fame is no plant that grows on mortal soil,
Nor in the glistering foil
Set off to th'world, nor in broad rumour lies,
But lives and spreads aloft by those pure eyes
And perfect witness of all-judging Jove;
As he pronounces lastly on each deed,
Of so much fame in Heav'n expect thy meed."
O fountain Arethuse, and thou honour'd flood,
Smooth-sliding Mincius, crown'd with vocal reeds,

That strain I heard was of a higher mood.
But now my oat proceeds,
And listens to the Herald of the Sea,
That came in Neptune's plea.
He ask'd the waves, and ask'd the felon winds,
"What hard mishap hath doom'd this gentle swain?"
And question'd every gust of rugged wings
That blows from off each beaked promontory.
They knew not of his story;
And sage Hippotades their answer brings,
That not a blast was from his dungeon stray'd;
The air was calm, and on the level brine
Sleek Panope with all her sisters play'd.
It was that fatal and perfidious bark,
Built in th'eclipse, and rigg'd with curses dark,
That sunk so low that sacred head of thine.
Next Camus, reverend sire, went footing slow,
His mantle hairy, and his bonnet sedge,
Inwrought with figures dim, and on the edge
Like to that sanguine flower inscrib'd with woe.
"Ah! who hath reft," quoth he, "my dearest pledge?"
Last came, and last did go,
The Pilot of the Galilean lake;
Two massy keys he bore of metals twain
(The golden opes, the iron shuts amain).
He shook his mitred locks, and stern bespake:
"How well could I have spar'd for thee, young swain,
Enow of such as for their bellies' sake
Creep and intrude, and climb into the fold?
Of other care they little reck'ning make
Than how to scramble at the shearers' feast
And shove away the worthy bidden guest.
Blind mouths! that scarce themselves know how to hold

A sheep-hook, or have learn'd aught else the least
That to the faithful herdman's art belongs!
What recks it them? What need they? They are sped;
And when they list their lean and flashy songs
Grate on their scrannel pipes of wretched straw,
The hungry sheep look up, and are not fed,
But, swoll'n with wind and the rank mist they draw,
Rot inwardly, and foul contagion spread;
Besides what the grim wolf with privy paw
Daily devours apace, and nothing said,
But that two-handed engine at the door
Stands ready to smite once, and smite no more".
Return, Alpheus: the dread voice is past
That shrunk thy streams; return, Sicilian Muse,
And call the vales and bid them hither cast
Their bells and flow'rets of a thousand hues.
Ye valleys low, where the mild whispers use
Of shades and wanton winds, and gushing brooks,
On whose fresh lap the swart star sparely looks,
Throw hither all your quaint enamel'd eyes,
That on the green turf suck the honied showers
And purple all the ground with vernal flowers.
Bring the rathe primrose that forsaken dies,
The tufted crow-toe, and pale jessamine,
The white pink, and the pansy freak'd with jet,
The glowing violet,
The musk-rose, and the well attir'd woodbine,
With cowslips wan that hang the pensive head,
And every flower that sad embroidery wears;
Bid amaranthus all his beauty shed,
And daffadillies fill their cups with tears,
To strew the laureate hearse where Lycid lies.
For so to interpose a little ease,

Let our frail thoughts dally with false surmise.
Ay me! Whilst thee the shores and sounding seas
Wash far away, where'er thy bones are hurl'd;
Whether beyond the stormy Hebrides,
Where thou perhaps under the whelming tide
Visit'st the bottom of the monstrous world,
Or whether thou, to our moist vows denied,
Sleep'st by the fable of Bellerus old,
Where the great vision of the guarded mount
Looks toward Namancos and Bayona's hold:
Look homeward Angel now, and melt with ruth;
And, O ye dolphins, waft the hapless youth.
Weep no more, woeful shepherds, weep no more,
For Lycidas, your sorrow, is not dead,
Sunk though he be beneath the wat'ry floor;
So sinks the day-star in the ocean bed,
And yet anon repairs his drooping head,
And tricks his beams, and with new spangled ore
Flames in the forehead of the morning sky:
So Lycidas sunk low, but mounted high
Through the dear might of him that walk'd the waves;
Where, other groves and other streams along,
With nectar pure his oozy locks he laves,
And hears the unexpressive nuptial song,
In the blest kingdoms meek of joy and love.
There entertain him all the Saints above,
In solemn troops, and sweet societies,
That sing, and singing in their glory move,
And wipe the tears for ever from his eyes.
Now, Lycidas, the shepherds weep no more:
Henceforth thou art the Genius of the shore,
In thy large recompense, and shalt be good
To all that wander in that perilous flood.

> Thus sang the uncouth swain to th'oaks and rills,
> While the still morn went out with sandals gray;
> He touch'd the tender stops of various quills,
> With eager thought warbling his Doric lay;
> And now the sun had stretch'd out all the hills,
> And now was dropp'd into the western bay;
> At last he rose, and twitch'd his mantle blue:
> To-morrow to fresh woods, and pastures new.

Introduction

Background and Text. Lycidas first appeared in a 1638 collection of elegies entitled Justa Edouardo King Naufrago. This collection commemorated the death of Edward King, a collegemate of Milton's at Cambridge who drowned when his ship sank off the coast of Wales in August, 1637. Milton volunteered or was asked to make a contribution to the collection. The present edition follows the copy of Poems of Mr. John Milton (1645) in the Rauner Collection at Dartmouth College known as Hickmott 172. Milton made a few significant revisions to Lycidas after 1638. These revisions are noted as they occur.

Form and Structure. The structure of Lycidas remains somewhat mysterious. J. Martin Evans argues that there are two movements with six sections each that seem to mirror each other. Arthur Barker believes that the body of Lycidas is composed of three movements that run parallel in pattern. That is, each movement begins with an invocation, then explores the conventions of the pastoral, and ends with a conclusion to Milton's "emotional problem" (quoted in Womack).

Voice. Milton's headnote labels Lycidas a "monody": a lyrical lament for one voice. But the poem has several voices or personae, including the "uncouth swain" (the main narrator), who is "interrupted" first by Phoebus

(Apollo), then Camus (the river Cam, and thus Cambridge University personified), and the "Pilot of the Galilean lake" (St. Peter). Finally, a second narrator appears for only the last eight lines to bring a conclusion in ottava rima (see F. T. Prince). Before the second narrator enters, the poem contains the irregular rhyme and meter characteristic of the Italian canzone form. Canzone is essentially a polyphonic lyrical form, hence creating a serious conflict with the "monody." Milton may have meant "monody" in the sense that the poem should be regarded more as a story told completely by one person as opposed to a chorus. This person would presumably be the final narrator, who seemingly masks himself as the "uncouth swain." This concept of story-telling ties Lycidas closer to the genre of pastoral elegy.

Genre. Lycidas is a pastoral elegy, a genre initiated by Theocritus, also put to famous use by Virgil and Spenser. Christopher Kendrick asserts that one's reading of Lycidas would be improved by treating the poem anachronistically, that is, as if it was one of the most original pastoral elegies. Also, as already stated, it employs the irregular rhyme and meter of an Italian canzone. Stella Revard suggests that Lycidas also exhibits the influence of Pindaric odes, especially in its allusions to Orpheus, Alpheus, and Arethusa. The poem's arrangement in verse paragraphs and its introduction of various voices and personae are also features that anticipate epic structures.

Pastoral Perfection: Why Milton's Lycidas is a Classicist's Masterpiece?

John Milton was a poet, intellectual and civil servant who lived from 1608 to 1674 through times of dramatic religious and political instability and change. He is most renowned for being the author of Paradise Lost, a blank verse epic poem which is arguably one of the greatest works of English literature and momentous in a religious context due to his endeavour "to justifie the ways of God to man".

John Milton (1608–1674

Despite his incredible renown, much of his other poetic works haven't received as much attention in the public sphere. His poem Lycidas falls into this category. It is a pastoral elegy which was written in blank and rhymed verse in 1637 as part of a memorial collection for one of Milton's few university friends, Edward King. King was also at Christ's College, Cambridge, with Milton and wrote poetry too during his time there. Whilst travelling home to Ireland in August of 1637, King's ship struck a rock off the Welsh coast and was shipwrecked, the event in which King drowned. He was a reasonably successful academic at his college and worked as a tutor there but had ambitions to go into the church — a key feature in Milton's poem for him. The untimely death of this young peer at the college led to the dedication of a collection of elegies entitled Justa Edouardo King Naufrago in which a number of students and academics took part. The character of Lycidas, Milton's allegorical substitute for King, appears in the origins of the pastoral genre when Theocritus, in his 7th Idyll, presents him as a goatherd who is "a fine man of Cydonia" and was encountered "thanks to the Muses". Adopting this figure in the place of his departed friend was very suitable as Milton decided to dedicate to King's memory a pastoral elegy. There are many ways in which Milton shows his mastery of the literature and theology of the ancients through this poem yet detailing them all would be a lengthy task. In my view, the most valuable classical and poetic quality of Lycidas stems from Milton's ability to work within this academic genre and to innovate upon it in emotionally sensitive ways. These two actions testify to Milton's incredible ability, well worthy of his ongoing fame.

With this first skill — his workings within the pastoral genre — he manages to involve the ancient literary tropes whilst maintaining a striking sensitivity. Milton involves a plethora of pastoral and other classical imagery in the formats of nature, pastoral activities, eroticism and epic poetry.

The references to the natural and idyllic world are consistent with the expectations of a pastoral poem. This can be seen in Milton's details in the early lines concerning the "Laurels", "Myrtles", "Ivy" and "Berries". From this starting point, Milton has established the pastoral environment and this theme is continued until the end of the elegy with the gathering of flowers for the assumed cortège. Here, the narrator asks for "Flourets of a thousand hues", "the rathe Primrose", the "white Pink and the Pansie freakt with jeat" as well as the "glowing Violet", "Musk-rose" and "Cowslips". The choice of flora represents the expected varieties inherited from the pastoral legacy yet with the offerings of an idyllic British landscape. This merging of the content of the classical with that of the 'English garden' offers a merging of the classical as well as King and Milton's ideals of nature. This brings the reverence of the classical into the application of the everyday — a feature which reflects solemnly on the everyday and inconsequential passing of a young man. The reflection of nature and the banality of human mortality seen in Malherbe's, 1599, "Rose elle a vécu" could have been a contemporary influence for Milton in this respect. Although the inclusion of nature is necessary for it to be a pastoral poem, Milton's very local scale adds to the pathos felt by the reader for the rather insignificant King. This sympathy is a vast improvement on classical pastoral for modern readers as often we can be left feeling cold by the very glorious yet anodyne environment such as we find in Theocritus 1ˢᵗ Idyll. It is surprising for us that the narrated story of Daphnis' death details how a number of figures from mythology visit him who are devoid of any sympathy and comfort for Daphnis in his last moments. Therefore, Milton's efforts to induce our sympathy for the poem's situation is a sensitive improvement upon the legacy of pastoral elegy.

Milton embodies the pastoral setting through the activities the narrator and Lycidas take part in. Portraying himself as the "uncouth swain", him and Lycidas "were nurst upon the self-same hill". Their partnership in their pastoral life continues as, "together both", they "fed the same flock". The narrator stresses that "the Rural ditties were not mute" and "temper'd to th'oaten flute" both "Rough Satyrs danc'd" with "Fauns with clov'n heel". Again, a staple feature of the pastoral genre is the art of the herdsmen and their peaceful musical contests. Depicted by Virgil in his Eclogues, these activities were clearly a necessary branding for the pastoral genre but soon developed the opportunity for allegory by their dream-like irrelevance. Milton picks up this idea and runs with it, mirroring all the pastoral activities with his and King's life at Cambridge. This parallel is furthered when "Camus, reverend Sire" asks who has "reft my dearest pledge". Camus is the deified embodiment of the River Cam and is a striking innovation from Milton to once again link this idyllic genre with his peer's lifestyle. Milton makes another meaningful parallel which was further used by other renaissance poets between the role of the shepherd and a religious leader. King had proposed that his mission was to join the church and therefore act as a herdsman for his congregation which Milton denotes when they both "drove a field". This religious adaptation has more profound impacts to be later explored.

Lycidas contains a faint eroticism in line with much pastoral poetry. The Eclogues contain much erotic turmoil and the pastoral genre is certainly a setting for sexualised content as we can see in the storylines of the 'Greek Novels'. Milton develops a subtle erotic environment in certain parts of the poem by focusing on Lycidas' youth and face. Such a decision finds reflection in the erotic elements of Sappho's poetry which follows similar focal points of youth and facial beauty. Lycidas' narrator laments the "remorseless deep clos'd o'er the head of your lov'd Lycidas" and the event that "sunk so low that sacred head of yours". Likewise Sappho, when discussing the girls of her circle, focuses on "your fine cheeks" which deserve "rich gifts" and requests one to "release that fineness in your irises". Milton's narrator refers to the dead man as the "young Lycidas" — a "young swain" — who he depicts as a "hapless youth". In the same way Sappho craves youth as shown in her poetic advice that "there is no other girl than she, Bridegroom" and encourages her "girls" to "chase the violet-bosomed Muses' bright gifts". Youth as beauty is portrayed in a different light when she laments that "age weighs heavily on me" and that she "can't stand being the old one any longer". Milton has worked his material into one that is especially suitable to the realm of pastoral elegy and pulls in other generic erotic themes to display a personal endearment to King in the light of his sudden death.

King's memorial poem is also infused with themes from the lofty world of epic. The genre of pastoral poetry received the legacy of epic and this is also necessarily registered by Milton. Most explicitly, Milton focuses on the epic trope of inauspicious boats. From the Homeric views towards the boat that brought Paris to Greece and Helen off to Troy and the ominous sentiments of the collapse of the golden age from the vessel used in Apollonius' Argonautica, the criticism and suspicion surrounding sea-faring vessels received lots of attention. This was a feature which warranted imitation in Catullus 64 in which Ariadne prays that "Almighty Jove, if only in that first of times, Cecropian hulls had never touched the Cnossian shore". And again, Euripides' Medea is testament to this view when the nurse laments "Would God the Argo had never winged the seas To Colchis through the blue Symplegades: No shaft of riven pine in Pelion's glen Shaped that first oar-blade in the hands of men...". Similarly Medea voices her own hatred of the boat in the Argonautica:"O my mother, take this farewell from me as I go far hence. Farewell Chalciope, and all my home. Would that the sea, stranger, had dashed thee to pieces, before you came to the Colchian land!" In the same vein in Lycidas, after the narrator has been assured by Hippotades that "The Ayre was calm ... on the level brine", he curses the cause of his loss — "It was that fatall and perfidious Bark Built in th'eclipse, and rigg'd with curses dark, That sunk so low that sacred head of thine". Milton has applied this classical trope of resentment around sea-faring, displayed throughout much ancient literature, for such a fitting situation to convey all the anger and bitterness of his personal grief.

The next section covers the ways in which Milton has developed areas in order to express a religious purpose. Not only are there many biblical references in the poem, but he has adapted classical poetic concepts in order to express his theological message. In this sense, I shall first look at Milton's use of poetic fame.

Reading any poetry that comes under the banner of classics, you will encounter the pursuit of fame. Whether affected and insincere or the veritable inspiration for a poet's efforts, many authors — particularly elegists — present this as a key concern. At the end of Amores 1, Ovid famously states: "each man's fame protects him as he deserves. So, even when the final flame has consumed me, I shall live and a considerable part of me will survive." Callimachus denotes that he too has achieved fame that has even reached the king of gods: "With that he concluded, and in response I said, "Lycidas my friend, the Muses have taught me too many good songs as I tended my herd in the hills, and their reputation may even have reached the throne of Zeus". As is evident, fame and its achievement is a key issue for such poets and likewise for Milton's narrator. In the light of Lycidas' premature death, the narrator, suspicious and disillusioned, asks: "What boots it with incessant care To tend the homely, slighted shepherd's trade, And strictly meditate the thankless Muse?" He finally claims that "Fame is the spur that the clear spirit doth raise (That last infirmity of noble mind) To scorn delights and live laborious days;" but even this is pointless as up "Comes the blind Fury with th'abhorred shears, And slits the thin-spun life." It is here that Milton develops a foothold for his religious message and has Apollo answer the narrator that the mortality displayed in Lycidas is not the case with 'fame': "Fame is no plant that grows on mortal soil, Nor in the glistering foil". This is in accordance with the claims of ancient poets yet Milton develops his sense of 'fame' with a christian slant — reflecting the promise of an afterlife — which places it with a certain religious worth, ensuring Lycidas' (therefore King's) legacy and endurance — "Of so much fame in Heav'n expect thy meed".

Pastoral poetry is witness to much thinly-veiled criticism of competitors. We can see this in Theocritus' seventh Idyll where the first person character of Simichidas has a go at "the builder who strives to produce a house as high as Mt. Oromedon and those fledgelings of the Muses who vainly struggle to crow in rivalry with the Chian bard". Milton picks up this idea of criticism, enabling it into an opportunity to criticise the state of religious leaders in the church at that time. St Peter is the mouthpiece of this criticism for the worthless shepherds — "What recks it them? What need they? They are sped; And when they list their lean and flashy songs Grate on their scrannel pipes of wretched straw, The hungry sheep look up, and are not fed". St Peter is further angered that it is Lycidas who has died and Milton generates pathos by the saint's anger towards those who have survived, highlighting further their unsuitability for their vocation: "How well could I have spar'd for thee, young swain, Enow of such as for their bellies' sake Creep and intrude, and climb into the fold?" This leads into the possibly discomforting christian idea of a final judgement and retribution as those "Blind mouths! that scarce themselves know how to hold A sheep-hook" will be met by "that two-handed engine at the door Stands ready to smite once, and smite no more." Considered the most confusing and debatable couplet of the poem, one can make an easier link with this statement and another of Milton's pastoral developments — the Garden of Eden. In fact, this thematic connection was often drawn by other renaissance Christian poets. This renowned couplet allows for a deeper connection to be made between the idyllic pastoral background of the poetic genre and the legendary garden of Eden because of the orthodox and wider Christian links concerning the biblical phenomenon of the 'flaming sword'. In Genesis 3:24, we read that a cherub was set outside the entrance to the garden of Eden with a flaming sword after Adam and Eve's banishment. In the Eastern Orthodox tradition, it is believed that after Christ's resurrection, this flaming sword was removed from preventing access back into the paradisaical garden. So therefore, although the couplet sheds little explicit light as to what this "engine" is referring to, the illusory value invites deeper interpretation and develops a stronger link with the pastoral setting and the natural setting of great worth to Judeo-Christian traditions.

Throughout the vast majority of the poem, Milton keeps within the setting and restrictions of his chosen genre and all his innovations for his 'Christian message' purposes are subtle and in character with pastoral expectations. However, towards the end of the poem, the arrival of St Peter, "The Pilot of the Galilean lake", makes a stark change in the poem's atmosphere and direction. It is not a lament or a competition or an eroticised story from mythology. Rather, St Peter's words carry the weight of a threat and a fearful evaluation of a society crammed with immoral religious leaders. His reference to the work of a personified evil — "Besides what the grim wolf with privy paw Daily devours apace" — imbues the poem with a sinister tone rarely noted in previous pastoral. The saint's presence and proclamation are depicted as so frightening that the narrator needs to ask the deities of "Alpheus" and the "Sicilian Muse" to "return" as "the dread voice is past That shrunk thy streams". This is a shattering of the pastoral mirage as seen in no other master of the genre. I believe that this is Milton's greatest innovation in the genre for the shocking fracture of the poem's atmosphere invites inquiry from the reader. Although many of the proposed messages have a lack of clarity in their meaning, by breaking the form, Milton forces the reader to look for other senses in the poem as it is no longer dictated by pastoral requirements. It is then here that we may pick up on the possible purpose of Milton's to display a certain religious worth in his poem. In its pastoral sense, Lycidas, is the most fitting way to remember King, but once the setting is broken, the other aspects, particularly the warning to the church, find their way to the fore in the area of the poem which breaks its content's restrictions. This effect was missed by the 18th century poet Samuel Johnson who states that the "representation may be allegorical" yet "the true meaning is so uncertain and remote, that it is never sought, because it cannot be known when it is found".

Overall, Milton shows his awareness of the classical genres he has chosen to write in and proves his ability by the sensitivity with which he implements these tropes, not to the disadvantage of the power of his poem. Again, Johnson appears to be ignorant to this when he writes that "in this poem ... there is no art, for there is nothing new ". Lycidas is not crowded with self-conscious posturing or excessively niche references — it is incredibly moving. Milton masters an ability to induce pathos by mingling the reverence of life (felt through his idyllic pastoral and deified backdrop) with its insignificance expressed in the narrator's grief alongside humbling 'small-world' features. This seems like such a fitting way to mark the passing of an educated, yet unknown, beloved friend who's demise seemed cruelly early and unremembered.

Concerning his religious aims, his innovations promote a challenging reading, reflecting his challenging of the current state of the church. Johnson again is critical of his combination of King's death — "trifling fictions" — and the Christian faith, as such combinations are "indecent, and at least approach impiety", sentiments which he believed "the writer to not have been conscious". Johnson here has missed the quality of the poem. Milton's creative adaptations develop the links between his message and the pastoral genre, saving the most frightening and severe aspect of the whole work for the most reverent purpose.

So, I can only encourage people to go off and read Lycidas. It makes for good reading not only from a 'classical-literary-appreciation' point of view but mainly from its honest exploration of mortality. Milton does not eulogise over King through the poem but conveys the distress caused by the passing of a peer and one with whom he is unsure over his actual relationship. His confusion and resentment are powerful as well as the sympathy invoked towards King. Mastery of his genre and the legacy within which he writes is displayed throughout the poem. Possibly most importantly, it is the manner in which he integrates his religious message offering his comfort for the human condition — hope for immortality — which makes for the most powerful reading.

Important lines form Lycidas:
But the fair guerdon when we hope to find,
And think to burst out into sudden blaze,
Comes the blind Fury with th'abhorred shears,
And slits the thin-spun life. 73-76
Explanation:
These lines express the speaker's frustration and grief over Lycidas's death. He reflects on how Lycidas had great

potential and hoped to achieve remarkable things ("fair guerdon"). Just as someone expects to burst into success and recognition ("sudden blaze"), Lycidas's life is tragically cut short. The unexpectedness and finality of death are emphasized by the contrast between the anticipated "blaze" and the abrupt ending.

Key terms:

• Guerdon: Reward, usually for achievement or merit.

• Blaze: Sudden burst of light or glory.

• Fury: In Greek mythology, the Erinyes were vengeful goddesses associated with violence and retribution. Here, "Fury" is personified as a blind force representing death.

• Shears: An instrument used for cutting, symbolizing the finality of death.

• Thin-spun life: A metaphor for the fragility of human life.

"He knew Himself to sing, and build the lofty rhyme./ He must not float upon his watery bier/ Unwept, and welter to the parching wind," (Lines 105-109)

Explanation:

The lines you provided are from John Milton's elegy "Lycidas," lamenting the death of a young poet named Edward King. Let's break down the meaning of each line and the overall message:

Line 105: "He knew Himself to sing, and build the lofty rhyme."

• This line establishes that Lycidas was not only talented but also self-aware of his poetic ability.

• "Sing" and "build the lofty rhyme" both refer to his skill in crafting poetry, likely of a grand and ambitious style.

Line 106: "He must not float upon his watery bier"

• Here, "watery bier" is a metaphor for the ocean, where Lycidas drowned.

• A bier is a platform on which a corpse is placed before burial, emphasizing the finality of Lycidas's death.

Line 107: "Unwept, and welter to the parching wind,"

• "Unwept" indicates a fear that Lycidas might be forgotten and unmourned.

• "Welter" means to toss about violently, suggesting the image of his body being battered by the ocean waves.

• "Parching wind" adds a layer of harshness and discomfort to the already bleak image.

Line 108: "Without the meed of some melodious tear."

• "Meed" means a deserved reward or offering.

• A "melodious tear" is a metaphor for a poem, specifically a lament or elegy written in his honor.

• This line emphasizes the importance of poetry as a form of commemoration and mourning.

Overall Message:

These lines express the speaker's deep grief for Lycidas and their belief that he deserves to be remembered and honored through poetry. They argue that his talent and potential merit a "melodious tear," ensuring his legacy isn't lost to the harshness of nature and oblivion.

Additional Points:

• The reference to Lycidas's own ability to "build the lofty rhyme" creates a sense of tragic irony, highlighting the loss of his potential.

• The speaker's passionate call for a "melodious tear" sets the stage for the rest of the poem, which itself becomes a fulfillment of that wish.

"Look homeward Angel now, and melt with ruth:/

And, O ye Dolphins', waft the hapless youth." (Lines 163-164) –

This line appeals to divine intervention and suggests faith as a source of comfort Explain?

Interpretation:

• Look homeward Angel: The speaker implores a guardian angel to return to its heavenly home. This implies that the angel has been present on Earth, potentially protecting Lycidas, the drowned young shepherd.

• And melt with ruth: The speaker asks the angel to be moved by compassion ("ruth") for Lycidas' unfortunate fate.

• And, O ye Dolphins', waft the hapless youth: The speaker pleads with the dolphins to transport Lycidas' body safely back to his home.

Symbolic Interpretation:

• Angel: The angel can represent various interpretations. It could be a literal guardian angel, a symbol of divine protection, or even a metaphor for Lycidas' own soul ascending to heaven.

• Melting with ruth: This can signify either the angel's own sorrow for Lycidas or its power to intercede with God on his behalf.

• Dolphins: In mythology, dolphins were often associated with guidance and safe passage, making them symbolic vessels for carrying Lycidas home.

Faith as Comfort:

By appealing to the angel and dolphins, the speaker expresses hope for something beyond human control. This act of faith, even in the face of immense grief, offers comfort in the possibility of divine intervention and a peaceful afterlife for Lycidas.

However, it's important to note that there's a subtle ambiguity in the lines.

•Is the speaker genuinely hopeful, or is this a desperate plea in the face of tragedy?

•Does the poem ultimately offer solace through faith, or does it highlight the limitations of human control and the unknown nature of the afterlife?

Milton leaves these questions open to interpretation, inviting readers to engage with the complex nature of faith and grief.

"Fame is no plant that grows on mortal soil,/Nor in the glistering foil/Set off to th'world, nor in broad rumour lies," (Lines 70-72) - This line challenges the idea of earthly fame and suggests that true recognition comes from God Explain?

Ans: John Milton's poem "Lycidas," express a clear skepticism towards worldly fame and recognition. Let's unpack the points further:

1. Mortality of earthly fame: "Fame is no plant that grows on mortal soil" emphasizes the fleeting nature of earthly recognition. By calling it a "plant" that grows on "mortal soil," the speaker highlights its impermanence, suggesting that fame based on earthly achievements withers and dies along with our mortality.

2. Superficiality of appearances: "Nor in the glistering foil/Set off to th'world" criticizes the shallowness of outward appearances and public perception. "Glistering foil" symbolizes a superficial, attention-grabbing facade that may attract immediate recognition but lacks depth and substance.

3. Impermanence of rumors: "Nor in broad rumour lies" dismisses the fleeting and unreliable nature of popular chatter. Rumors may bring temporary fame, but they are often inaccurate, distorted, and quickly forgotten.

By contrasting these earthly sources of fame with the "Immortal Amaranth" mentioned later in the poem, the speaker suggests that true recognition comes from God and endures beyond our mortal existence. This aligns with religious and philosophical perspectives that see true value in spiritual growth and connection with a higher power rather than fleeting, earthly achievements.

It's important to note that not everyone interprets these lines in the same way. Some might focus on the critique of shallow fame without necessarily attributing true recognition to God. Ultimately, the poem invites introspection and individual interpretation on the value and meaning of true recognition.

Ay me! Whilst thee the shores and sounding Seas

Wash far away, where ere thy bones are hurld, (Lines 154-155)

Explanation:

These lines express the speaker's deep grief and anguish over the death of Lycidas. He imagines Lycidas's body being tossed around by the waves of the vast and powerful sea, far away from any land.

"Ay me!": This is an exclamation of lament, expressing the speaker's sorrow and despair.

"Whilst thee the shores and sounding Seas/Wash far away": This personifies the sea, imagining it as an active force that is carrying Lycidas's body away. The use of "sounding Seas" emphasizes the vastness and power of the ocean, which seems to dwarf and isolate Lycidas.

"where ere thy bones are hurld": This further emphasizes the sense of Lycidas being lost and alone at sea. The image of his bones being "hurled" suggests a lack of control and finality.

Overall, these lines create a powerful image of Lycidas's isolation and the speaker's helplessness in the face of death.

Additional notes:

The line "sounding Seas" is an example of Milton's use of alliteration, which can create a sense of rhythm and emphasis.

The image of the sea is also significant in the poem because it is often associated with death and the underworld in mythology and literature.

These lines are part of a larger section of the poem where the speaker is lamenting the loss of Lycidas and questioning the meaning of life and death.

"And now the sun had stretch'd out all the hills,

And now was dropp'd into the western bay;

At last he rose, and twitch'd his mantle blue:

To-morrow to fresh woods, and pastures new."

Lines 190 - 193

Explanation:

These lines are from the concluding part of John Milton's pastoral elegy "Lycidas." Let's break down the lines:

1. "And now the sun had stretch'd out all the hills": This line indicates the passage of time as the sun has spread its light across the landscape, covering all the hills. It suggests the completion of a day or a phase.

2. "And now was dropp'd into the western bay": The sun has descended and disappeared into the western horizon, signifying the end of the day as it sets over the sea.

3. "At last he rose, and twitch'd his mantle blue": This refers to the rising of a new day. The sun, personified here, "rises" and seems to adjust or shake off its "mantle," symbolizing the morning sky. The "mantle blue" likely refers to the color of the sky at dawn.

4. "To-morrow to fresh woods, and pastures new": The speaker expresses anticipation for the coming day. The sun, having set, is expected to rise again tomorrow. The phrase "fresh woods, and pastures new" suggests a sense of renewal and the promise of new experiences or opportunities. It reflects a hopeful and forward-looking attitude.

In these lines, Milton uses the imagery of the sun's cycle to convey the cyclical nature of life and the idea of renewal and new beginnings, echoing the broader themes of the poem.

Lycidas as Pastoral Elegy

Introduction

"Lycidas" is a renowned pastoral elegy composed by John Milton, one of the most eminent English poets of the 17th century. Published in 1638, the poem serves as a lamentation for Edward King, a fellow student at Cambridge who tragically drowned in the Irish Sea. The elegy is named after the shepherd Lycidas, a character from ancient Greek pastoral poetry, and it draws upon the conventions of the pastoral genre while also incorporating elements of the elegiac tradition.

What is a Pastoral Elegy?

A pastoral elegy is a type of poem that combines the conventions of pastoral poetry with the themes of mourning and loss. Pastoral poetry typically features idealized settings of rural life, with shepherds and shepherdesses as characters. Elegies, on the other hand, are poems that lament the death of a person.

How does Lycidas fit the Pastoral Elegy genre?

• Setting: The poem is set in an idealized Arcadia, a mythical land of peace and beauty.

- Characters: The speaker and Lycidas are both shepherds, representing Milton and King, respectively.

- Themes: The poem explores themes of grief, loss, the transience of life, and the hope for consolation and immortality.

1. Pastoral Elements:

- Shepherd Imagery: Milton employs the pastoral tradition by presenting the characters as shepherds, a common motif in pastoral poetry. Lycidas, the deceased friend, is depicted as a shepherd who has met an untimely death.

- Nature and Landscape: The poem is set against the backdrop of nature, using vivid descriptions of the pastoral landscape. The pastoral scenes symbolize both the idyllic and fleeting nature of life.

2. Elegiac Elements:

- Lamentation: As an elegy, "Lycidas" is fundamentally an expression of grief. Milton mourns the loss of his friend, exploring themes of death, mortality, and the transience of life.

- **Consolation:** The poem seeks to console the mourners by addressing the idea of immortality and the possibility of life after death. Milton draws on Christian themes to provide comfort in the face of tragedy.

3. Religious and Mythological Allusions:

- Biblical References: Milton, a deeply religious poet, incorporates biblical allusions into the elegy. The poem reflects his theological concerns, including references to the parable of the talents and the biblical story of King David.

- Classical Allusions: Milton draws on classical mythology, incorporating references to the Muses, Proteus, and other figures from Greek and Roman tradition. These allusions enrich the poem's intellectual depth.

4. Invocation and Allegory:

• Invocation of the Muse: Following the classical tradition, Milton begins with an invocation to the Muse, seeking inspiration for his elegy. This invocation connects "Lycidas" to classical epics and reinforces its literary lineage.

• Allegorical Elements: The poem contains allegorical elements, with characters representing real individuals and abstract concepts. Lycidas, for instance, is not just a shepherd but symbolizes the deceased friend and the broader theme of the loss of virtuous individuals.

5. Elegy as Critique:

• Social and Political Commentary: "Lycidas" is not merely a personal lament but also a reflection on the political and ecclesiastical turmoil of Milton's time. The poem addresses issues such as corruption within the clergy and the state of the Church of England.

6. Structure and Style:

• Miltonic Verse: The poem is written in a variation of the Spenserian stanza, a nine-line verse form employed by Edmund Spenser. This choice reflects Milton's engagement with earlier poetic traditions and showcases his mastery of poetic form.

• Elevated Style: Milton's language is elevated and complex, characteristic of his broader poetic style. The poem is replete with metaphors, similes, and intricate wordplay.

"Lycidas" stands as a multifaceted work that transcends the boundaries of pastoral and elegy. It serves not only as a memorial for a departed friend but also as a meditation on life, death, faith, and the challenges facing society. By skillfully blending classical, biblical, and personal elements, Milton creates a rich and enduring piece of literature that continues to captivate readers with its emotional depth and intellectual resonance.

Themes of Lycidas written by John Milton

"Lycidas" by John Milton explores several themes that are both personal and reflective of broader concerns of the time. The poem, written in the pastoral and elegiac tradition, delves into themes such as:

1. Grief and Loss:

• The central theme of "Lycidas" is the deep sense of grief and loss experienced by the poet upon the death of his friend, Edward King (Lycidas). The poem serves as a powerful expression of mourning and lamentation.

2. Mortality and the Transience of Life:

• The poem reflects on the fragility and brevity of human life. Through the death of Lycidas, Milton contemplates the transient nature of existence and the inevitability of death.

3. Nature and the Idyllic Pastoral Landscape:

• The pastoral setting of the poem provides an idyllic backdrop, emphasizing the harmonious relationship between humanity and nature. The descriptions of the pastoral landscape evoke a sense of beauty and tranquility.

4. Christian Faith and Redemption:

• Milton, a devout Christian, weaves religious themes throughout the poem. He explores the concept of divine providence, suggesting that despite the apparent injustice of Lycidas's death, there is a greater plan at work. The poem contemplates the idea of redemption and the possibility of an afterlife.

5. Intellectual and Poetic Tradition:

• "Lycidas" engages with classical and biblical traditions. Milton invokes classical mythology, draws on biblical allusions, and employs the pastoral genre, showcasing his erudition and literary mastery. The poem is a testament to the poet's awareness of and reverence for literary and intellectual traditions.

6. Critique of Corruption and Degeneration:

• The poem contains social and political commentary, critiquing the corruption within the clergy and the state of the Church of England. Milton expresses concern about the moral degeneration of institutions and individuals in his contemporary society.

7. Consolation and Hope:

• Amidst the grief, Milton seeks to provide consolation and hope. He explores the idea that death is not the end, and there is the potential for spiritual renewal and eternal life. The poem reflects a Christian optimism that transcends earthly sorrows.

8. Friendship and Commemoration:

• "Lycidas" serves as a tribute to Milton's friendship with Edward King. The poem memorializes the deceased friend and expresses the enduring impact of friendship, even in the face of death.

9. Elegy as Artistic Expression:

• The poem itself becomes a reflection on the art of elegy. Milton uses the elegiac form not only to mourn but also to explore the possibilities and limitations of poetic expression in the face of profound loss.

10. Personal and Political Suffering:

• While lamenting the death of his friend, Milton also uses "Lycidas" to express his personal and political views.

The poem addresses the turbulent times of the 17th century, touching upon issues such as the corruption within the Church and the broader societal challenges.

"Lycidas" is a rich and complex work that weaves together these themes, offering readers a profound meditation on life, death, faith, and the enduring power of art. The poem's ability to resonate on personal, intellectual, and spiritual levels contributes to its lasting significance in the canon of English literature.

****

CHAPTER FOUR

La Belle Dame sans Merci: A Ballad

La Belle Dame sans Merci: A Ballad

BY JOHN KEATS

O what can ail thee, knight-at-arms,
Alone and palely loitering?
The sedge has withered from the lake,
And no birds sing.
O what can ail thee, knight-at-arms,
So haggard and so woe-begone?
The squirrel's granary is full,
And the harvest's done.
I see a lily on thy brow,
With anguish moist and fever-dew,
And on thy cheeks a fading rose
Fast withereth too.
I met a lady in the meads,
Full beautiful—a faery's child,
Her hair was long, her foot was light,
And her eyes were wild.
I made a garland for her head,

And bracelets too, and fragrant zone;
She looked at me as she did love,
And made sweet moan
I set her on my pacing steed,
And nothing else saw all day long,
For sidelong would she bend, and sing
A faery's song.
She found me roots of relish sweet,
And honey wild, and manna-dew,
And sure in language strange she said—
'I love thee true'.
She took me to her Elfin grot,
And there she wept and sighed full sore,
And there I shut her wild wild eyes
With kisses four.
And there she lullèd me asleep,
And there I dreamed—Ah! woe betide!—
The latest dream I ever dreamt
On the cold hill side.
I saw pale kings and princes too,
Pale warriors, death-pale were they all;
They cried—'La Belle Dame sans Merci
Thee hath in thrall!'
I saw their starved lips in the gloam,
With horrid warning gapèd wide,
And I awoke and found me here,
On the cold hill's side.
And this is why I sojourn here,
Alone and palely loitering,
Though the sedge is withered from the lake,
And no birds sing.

About the poet:

Born of humble parentage in1795, was an English poet of the second generation of Romantic poets. From an early period his poetical bent displayed itself (studied Spenser, Chapman's Homer, and the Renaissance poets). His poems had been in publication for less than four years when he died of tuberculosis at the age of 25 (1821). They were indifferently received in his lifetime, but his fame grew rapidly after his death.[1] By the end of the century, he was placed in the canon of English literature, strongly influencing many writers of the Pre-Raphaelite Brotherhood; the Encyclopædia Britannica of 1888 called one ode "one of the final masterpieces".

1818. ***Endymion,*** ostensibly a legendary tale of the mythical lovers. The dominant theme is often transposed into an allegory of the poet's life and endeavor.

1820. ***Lamia, Isabella, The Eve of St. Agnes,*** This volume contains the Odes. Besides these must be mentioned the magnificient classic fragment *Hyperion,* and the wonderful and the haunting lines of *Autumn.*

Among not published in two volumes mentioned are:

1. The famous sonnet *On First Looking into Chapman's Homer* (1817).
2. *La Belle Dame Sans Merci*
3. *The Last Sonnet* (written on the voyage to Italy).

Literary Background:

The age of Keats is called 'the Romantic Age' in literature. Keats himself is one of the great Romantic poets of England. Therefore, inorder to understand his poetry it is essential to form an idea of the nature and characteristics of Romanticism.

English Romantic Movement was the movement in literature which started towards the end of the 18th century and continued till the thirties of the 19th century. It can be roughly dated from 1780 -1830. Also, there were poets of the 18th century who showed romantic tendencies in their writings before 1780s.

Romanticism is not a homogeneous group of tendencies, nor do all the Romantic poets form a homogeneous group. There are two generations of Romantics, and though there are some common tendencies between the two groups – tendencies derived from the general movement of Romanticism, -- there are also marked differences between the two groups.

Politically the earlier group (Wordsworth, Coleridge and Scott) were opponents of the French Revolution; Wordsworth and Coleridge were renegades, and Scott abhorred the Revolution. They set themselves up against the revolutionary ideals. The poetical reform of Wordsworth and Coleridge seeks its justification in a national idealism; they express a sympathetic interest in the poor peasant, but they also do not preach the revolutionary gospel of the rights of man. They settle down as conservatives and preach the cult of peace.

The second group of Romantics (Byron and Shelley) breathe a spirit of moral revolt; they refuse to recognize any tradition, and severely criticize a society based on conventional privileges. They are inspired by revolutionary ideals, and in their passion for liberty, rebel against all traditions; their poetry glows with passion, and they preach the cult of revolution.

What is Romanticism?

The term 'Romanticism' has been variously defined by various writers. Walter Pater calls it the "addition of strangeness to beauty" and Watts Dunton defines it as "the renaissance of wonder". Goethe contrasts Romanticism with Classicism and says, "Romanticism is a disease, Classicism is health." He thus emphasizes the imperfection and incompleteness of romantic art. Legouis and Cazamian emphasize both the emotional and imaginative aspects of romanticism and call it "an accentuated predominance of emotional life provoked and directed by the exercise of imaginative vision."All such definitions are partial, for they emphasize one or the other elements of this type of literature instead of giving a composite view.

Romanticism is a tendency found in all literatures and in all countries. Walter Pater and many other critics believe that there are mainly two types of art – romantic and classic or classical. Art is the creation of beauty. Romantic art tries to create the kind of beauty which is strange, mysterious and uncommon. Classical art, on the other hand, tries to create the kind of beauty which is orderly, familiar and significant. Romantic poetry is marked by an excess of imagination while classical poetry is marked by a sense of balance and proportion.

Critical Appreciation and Summary:

The title is taken from that of a poem by Alain Chartier, a French poet. The title has fascinated Keats and in the *Eve of St. Agnes,* he makes Prophyro sing this very song to awake his beloved. The title continued tohaunt the poet's imagination, till in a moment of inspiration he wrote this incomparable ballad.

The poem is set in a medieval setting. It tells of a knight who is wandering all alone on the cold hillside even though it is winter and no birds sings. He is pale and haggard, and his face shows signs of agony. On the poet's asking from him the cause of his misery, he replies that he met a beautiful lady, and fell in love with her. How he made love to her by presenting her gifts of flowers, and how he seated her on his horse. The lady made a show of love, took him to her cave and made love to him. At night he dreamed that pale warriors and kings were warning him that he was in the power of "La Belle Dame Sans Merci" (The Beautiful Lady without Mercy). When he woke up, he did not find the lady near him. Since then he has

been searching for her. That is why he is wandering about so pale and wretched.

The vagueness of the atmosphere makes the poem a document of horror and mystery. The merciless lady has literary has a mythological association that arouse a subdued horror. These suggestions of horror combined with the suggestion of the supernatural about the woman and knight errantry about the man, impart to the poem a medieval atmosphere, and atmosphere of medieval enchantment and chivalry.

The poem is thus a masterpiece from all points of view, from the view point of its technical mastry, its artistic economy, its romantic suggestiveness and simplicity. It was Keats's historic imagination, his 'negative capability', i.e., his ability to enter imaginatively into the life of other times and countries, that enabled him to vivify the Middle Ages so very effectively and accurately. However, it should be remembered that he has not a word to say about the ignorance, the ugliness, the poverty and the backwardness of those dark ages. His representation of the past, therefore, remains partial and one-sided. It is the vision of a romantic, a poet's dream, rather than the accurate rendering of a scientist or a historian. It was the romantic charm of the remote and the unknown that fascinated him rather than the actuality.

La Belle Dame Sans Merci Summary Line by Line

The speaker of the poem comes across a "knight at arms" alone, and apparently dying, in a field somewhere. He asks him what's going on, and the knight's answer takes up the rest of the poem. The knight says that he met a beautiful fairy lady in the fields. He started hanging out with her, making flower garlands for her, letting her ride on his horse, and generally flirting like knights do. Finally, she invited him back to her fairy cave. Sweet, thought the knight. But after they were through smooching, she "lulled" him to sleep, and he had a nightmare about all the knights and kings and princes that the woman had previously seduced – they were all dead. And then he woke up, alone, on the side of a hill somewhere.

Stanza 1, Lines 1-4

"O WHAT can ail thee, knight-at-arms,
 Alone and palely loitering?
 The sedge has wither'd from the lake,
 And no birds sing.

- The poem opens with a question: an unnamed speaker asks a "knight at arms" what's wrong, or what's "ail[ing]" him.
- Something is clearly wrong with the knight – he's "loitering" by himself around the edge of a lake, and he's "pale."
- The speaker says that the "sedge," or marsh plants, have all died out from around the lake, and "no birds sing."

So we're guessing that it's autumn or even early winter since all the birds have migrated, and the plants have "withered."

- The presence of the "knight at arms" reminds us of medieval fairy tales with knights and ladies in towers. We think that this is the response Keats intended

Stanza 2, Lines 5-8

"O what can ail thee, knight-at-arms,
So haggard and so woe-begone?
The squirrel's granary is full,
And the harvest's done.

- The first part of the stanza echoes the first line of the poem word-for-word. Apparently the knight doesn't answer immediately, so the unnamed speaker has to repeat the question.
- This time, we get two more adjectives to describe the knight: he's "haggard," or worn-out and tired-looking, and "woe-begone." The knight is obviously both sick and depressed.
- The last two lines of the stanza do more to set the scene: the squirrels have finished filling up their "granary," or storage of food for the winter, and the crops have already been harvested.
- We can now safely assume that it's late autumn.

Stanza 3, Lines 9-12

"I see a lily on thy brow

With anguish moist and fever-dew.
And on thy cheeks a fading rose
Fast withereth too."

- The speaker continues to address this sick, depressed "knight at arms." He asks about the "lily" on the knight's "brow," suggesting that the knight's face is pale like a lily.
- The knight's forehead is sweaty with "anguish" and with "fever," so he's obviously sick.
- The last two lines of the stanza describe how the healthy color is rapidly "fading" from the knight's cheeks.

Stanza 4, Lines 13-16

"I met a lady in the meads,
Full beautiful – a faery's child,
Her hair was long, her foot was light,
And her eyes were wild.

- This stanza changes point of view.
- All of a sudden, the knight answers the unnamed speaker's questions. So now the "I" is the knight, rather than the original speaker.
- The knight says that he met a beautiful, fairy-like "lady" in the "meads," or fields.
- She had long hair, was graceful, and had "wild" eyes. (We're not sure what "wild" eyes would look like, but apparently the knight thought it was attractive.)

Stanza 5, Lines 17-20

"I made a garland for her head,
*   And bracelets too, and fragrant zone;*
*   She look'd at me as she did love,*
*   And made sweet moan.*

- The knight made a flower wreath, or "garland," for the lady, along with flower "bracelets."
- The "fragrant zone" is a belt made of flowers.
- We get the idea that the knight decks out the maiden with flowers.
- "Fragrant zone" could also be a reference to her lady parts, which would make sense, given where the next two lines go.
- And where do the next two lines go? Well, the lady is "look[ing]" at the knight while "lov[ing]" and "moan[ing]," so we think that they two are having sex.

Stanza 6, Lines 21-24

"I set her on my pacing steed,
*   And nothing else saw all day long;*
*   For sidelong would she bend, and sing*
*   A faery's song.*

- The knight puts the lady on his horse (his "pacing steed") to take a ride. Yes, there might be sexy connotations to this line, too.
- The knight is so absorbed with his erotic encounter with this fairy lady that he doesn't notice anything else "all day long."
- The lady leans "sidelong," or sideways off of the horse and sings "fairy songs" to the knight.

Stanza 7, Lines 25-28

"She found me roots of relish sweet,
*   And honey wild and manna-dew;*
*   And sure in language strange she said,*
*   'I love thee true.'*

- The knight says that the fairy lady found him tasty roots, honey, and manna to eat ("of relish sweet").
- "Manna" is the food that the Jewish scriptures say that the Israelites ate when they were wandering around the desert after Moses freed them from slavery in Egypt. It's supposed to be food from heaven, so this word makes the fairy lady seem supernatural, if not actually divine.
- Alternatively, the association could be with the slavery from which the Israelites had just been freed. After all, the knight does become enslaved to the beautiful fairy lady. This allusion becomes even more potent when it's associated with the "honey wild" that the fairy lady fed the knight. (The Israelites were trying to find the Promised Land, which would flow with "milk and honey.")
- The fairy lady tells the knight that she loves him, but she says it "in language strange."
- He doesn't say what language it is, or how he's able to understand her. Maybe he's just hearing what he wants to hear, or maybe her magical influence has enabled him to understand her "language strange."

Stanza 8, Lines 29-32

"She took me to her elfin grot,
And there she wept and sigh'd full sore;
And there I shut her wild, wild eyes
With kisses four.

- The fairy lady takes the knight to her "elfin grot." "Elfin" just means having to do with elves, as any Tolkien fans probably figured. And a "grot" is a grotto, or cave.
- Once they're back at her fairy cave, she cries and sighs loudly. The knight doesn't say why she's crying, and we never find out – it's left to our imagination.
- The knight kisses her weepy eyes four times. (Why "four" kisses? Isn't "three" usually the magic number in fairy tales?)
- Again, her eyes are described as "wild," and this time it's repeated twice.

Stanza 9, Lines 33-36

"And there she lullèd me asleep,
And there I dream'd – ah! woe betide!
The latest dream I ever dream'd
On the cold hill's side.

- The fairy lady "lulls" the knight to sleep like a baby in her cave, and he starts to dream something.
- He interrupts himself with a dash – in line 34, and exclaims "Ah! woe betide!" because even the memory of the dream is horrible as he repeats it to the unnamed speaker.
- "Woe betide!" is an archaic exclamation used to express extreme grief or suffering. It was old-fashioned even

when Keats was writing.
- The knight's use of this expression emphasizes the medieval romance setting.
- The knight's dream in the fairy cave is the "latest," or last, dream he'll ever have.

Stanza 10, Lines 37-40

"I saw pale kings and princes too,
Pale warriors, death-pale were they all:
They cried, 'La belle Dame sans Merci
Hath thee in thrall!'

- The knight describes the dream he had: he saw "kings," "princes," and "warriors, and they were all "death pale." In fact, he repeats the word "pale" three times in two lines.
- This procession of "pale" men could be an allusion to the fourth horseman of the Apocalypse that gets described in the Book of Revelation in the Christian bible. The fourth horseman is Death, and he rides on a pale horse.
- The pale warriors, princes, and kings all cry out in unison that "La belle dame sans merci" has the knight "in thrall," or in bondage.
- Line 39 has the title of the poem in it, so it's time to translate it. The title is French and it translates to "the beautiful woman without mercy."

Stanza 11, Lines 41-44

"I saw their starved lips in the gloam

With horrid warning gapèd wide
And I awoke and found me here
On the cold hill's side.

- The knight continues to describe the pale warriors from his dream – in the "gloam," or dusk, all he can make out are their "lips."
- Their mouths are "starv'd" and hungry-looking, and their mouths are all open as they cry out their warning to the knight.
- The word "gloam" just means dusk or twilight, but it's no accident that Keats uses it – after all, "gloam" sounds a lot like "gloom."
- The knight wakes up from the dream alone and cold on the side of a hill.

Stanza 12, Lines 45-48

"And this is why I sojourn here
Alone and palely loitering,
Though the sedge is wither'd from the lake,
And no birds sing."

- The knight has finished his story. He tells the original, unnamed speaker, that this is why he's hanging out ("sojourn[ing]" and "loitering") by himself, even though it's so dismal outside.
- The knight repeats the unnamed speaker's words from the first stanza, so that the poem ends with almost exactly the same stanza with which it began.

Questions and Answers

1. Is the title of the Poem a good one? Why?

Yes, the title is a good one. It is appropriate because the knight-at-arms is enchanted by the beautiful lady and expresses his love for her but she instead of returning his love enslaves him and has no mercy for him.

2. Who is alone and palely loitering?

The Knight-at-arms is along and lingering with a pale face on the cold hillside.

3. What ails the knight?

The knight looks pale, sad and worried because the beautiful lady without pity has enslaved him and his fate will be like that of other pale kings and warriors.

4. Why did the lady charm the knight?

The enchantingly beautiful lady charmed the knight because she wanted to enslave him though she had no mercy for him.

5. What happened to the knight in the end?

The knight saw the pitiable condition of pale kings and warriors in the dream with their starved lips in the evening twilight. They cried that the beautiful lady "Hath thee in thrall!" He woke up as they warned him about his tragic fate. That is why the Knight is staying on the cold hill side alone looking pale and sad. Keats intentionally leaves the story at slightly mysterious note so that we may be left asking questions.

6. What is the theme of the poem?

The theme of the poem is unrequited love, and the pain and suffering of one who loves but is not loved in return. It is said that in writing this poem Keats was expressing his own feelings. He too loved but was not loved by Fanny Brawne.

7. What point of view is the poem written in? Who is its speaker(s)?

The poem is written in the first-person point of view. The poem is written as a dialogue between a knight and another man.

8. In the second stanza, what does the speaker say are reasons for the knight-at-arms to not "ail"?

The speaker says the "squirrel's granary is full," meaning it has been a slow fall, allowing much time for preparation. This concept is repeated in the second reason he gives, which is "the harvest's done."

9. Why does the lady weep and sigh in the poem's eighth stanza?

Answers may vary. Example: The lady weeps because she knows that while she loves the knight, they cannot be together since they are too different.

10. How does the French title translate into English?

The title translates into "The Beautiful Woman with No Mercy."

11. What does the speaker's dream suggest about the woman whom he has fallen in love with?

The pale people of the speaker's dreams warn him that he has fallen for a woman without pity, suggesting that she has left him for good, without consideration of his feelings.

12. Why do you believe the knight-at-arms is so sad?

Answers may vary. Example: One reason might be that when he awoke from his dream, the beautiful woman he had found and kissed was gone. Another reason might be his realization that the woman he had seen did not truly love him.

13. Explain the significance in the speaker's choice of words in the final stanza, especially "sojourn" and "palely."

The choice of "sojourn" suggests that the speaker is waiting for something, most likely his love. The choice of "palely" parallels the description he has given of the kings and princes in his dreams. This may infer that he has also fallen for la belle dame sans merci.

SHORT QUESTIONS AND ANSWERS

1. Which season is the poem set in?
Ans: The poem is set in the late autumn and the advent of the winter season.

2. Who is being addressed at the beginning of the poem?
Ans: The knight-at-arms is being addressed at the beginning of the poem.

3. Where did the knight meet the lady?
Ans: The knight met the lady in a meadow.

4. In which year was the poem composed?
Ans: The poem was composed in 1819.

5. What words did the lady utter?
Ans: The lady uttered in a strange language - "I love thee true".

1. What did the knight make for the lady?
Ans: The knight, in order to express his love, made a garland for the head, bracelets for the arms, and a girdle of flowers for the lady.

2. What did the lady give him in return?
Ans: In return for the gifts of the knight, the lady gave him relish sweet roots, wild honey, and manna dew i.e. nectar of the gods.

3. What did the lady do in her cave?
Ans: The fair lady took the knight to her fairy cave. In the cave, the lady wept bitterly and sight sorely. Being

overwhelmed by her expression of love, the knight kissed her wild and beautiful eyes. Then the lady lulled the knight to sleep.

4. Who did the knight see in his dream?

Ans: In his dream, the knight saw pale-faced kings, princes, and warriors who were the victim of the beautiful lady.

5. What was the lady known as?

Ans: The lady was known as 'La Belle Dame

Some Long Questions and Answers

1. What are the signs that show us that the knight is suffering?

Ans: The poem 'La Belle Dame Sans Merci' depicts the pain and suffering of the knight as he was betrayed by the beautiful lady without pity. He is loitering alone and pales on the cold and desolate hillside. His face looks wrinkled with deep pain and internal turmoil. His brow is pale like a lily and is moist and feverish caused by deep mental agony. Moreover, the bloom of the radiant cheeks of the knight faded like a fading rose. Again, it is the late autumn, an odd time of the year and the place he visits is not suitable to visit at that time. The sedge has withered away and the birds are also not singing. All these are the signs that clearly show us that the knight is suffering.

2. Give a description of the lady.

Ans: The lady in the poem 'La Belle Dame Sans Merci' is a very beautiful one. The knight met the lady in the meadow was pleasantly captivated by the charm and beauty of the lady. She was extremely beautiful with a face like a fairly's child, her hair was very long and she had attractive and wild eyes. Being nimble-footed, she attracted the knight with her movements. Her alluring long hair, the glance of her passionate eyes, and sweet moan enraptured the knight and eventually, he fell in love with the lady.

The knight, in order to express his love, made a garland for her head, bracelet for the lady. The lady was responsive to the knight's approach and her sweet moan reflected her love for the knight. The knight took her on his horseback and spent the whole day on a delightful ride. In response to the gifts of the knight, the knight, the lady offered him relish sweet roots, wild honey, and manna dew. She even expressed her love for the knight in a strange language. The fair lady took him to her fairy cave. In the cave, the lady wept bitterly and sight sorely. Being overwhelmed by her expression of love, the knight kissed her wild and beautiful eyes. Then the lady lulled her to sleep. But the lady ultimately betrayed the knight and left him all alone on a cold hillside.

3. Describe the dream of the knight.

Ans: In his sleep, the knight had a terrible dream. He dreamt of a number of kings, princes, and warriors who were looking pale and wearied. Their lips were dry and seemed to have been starved for a long period of time. They were the earlier victims of the lady who tormented them by her indifference and betrayal. They called the lady 'La Belle Dame Sans Merci' - which means 'the beautiful lady without pity' and warned the knight of the lady's apparent love, enslavement, and eventual deception. They further cautioned the knight that he would meet the same miserable fate as them. The startling dream woke the knight up and he found himself lying all alone on a cold hillside.

4.Why was the knight loitering about?

Ans: In the poem 'La Belle Dame Sans Merci' the poet John Keats speaks about a knight who was once enchanted by a beautiful lady and eventually got deceived by her apparent show of love. The knight happened to meet a beautiful lady in the meadow who was extremely beautiful and charming. Her alluring long hair nimble foot and glance of wild and passionate eyes enraptured the knight and eventually, he fell in love with the lady.

The knight, in order to express his love, made a garland for her head, a bracelet for the lady. The lady was responsive to the knight's approach and her sweet moan reflected her love for the knight. He spent the whole day in the delightful company of the lady and finally followed her to the fairy cave. She offered him relish sweet roots, wild honey, and manna dew and expressed her love for the knight in a strange language. In the cave, she displayed her emotion and lulled the knight to sleep.

In his sleep, the knight had a terrible dream. He dreamt of a number of kings, princes, and warriors who were looking pale and wearied. Their lips were dry and seemed to have been starved for a long period of time. They were the earlier victims of the lady who tormented them by her indifference and betrayal. They called the lady 'La Belle Dame Sans Merci' - which means 'the beautiful lady without pity' and warned the knight of the lady's apparent love, enslavement, and eventual deception. They further cautioned the knight that he would meet the same miserable fate as them. The startling dream woke the knight up and he found himself lying all alone on a cold hillside.

To his utter surprise, the knight realized that his dream turned into reality as the lady was not with him. He found it difficult to accept the reality - the betrayal of his lady love. Hence, he was forced to loiter about aimlessly with the anguish of unrequited love.

Previous Years Questions and Answers

1. What season is referred to in the poem 'La Belle Dame Sans Merci'?

Ans: Late autumn and the advent of the winter season is referred to in the poem. 'La Belle Dame Sans Merci'

2. Where did the knight meet the lady?

Ans: The knight met the lady in a meadow.

3. Who did the knight see in his dream?

Ans: In his dream, the knight saw pale-faced kings, princes, and warriors who were the victim of the beautiful lady.

4. Describe the experience of the knight in 'La Belle Dame Sans Merci'

Ans: See the above Qno. 2 (Give a suitable answer to the following.)

5. I saw their starved lips in the gloam.
With horrid warning gaped wide.
And I awoke and found me here,
On the cold hilTs side.

Ans: These lines have been taken from John Keat's poem "La Belle Dame Sans Merci" The poem deals with the pain of one who loves but is not loved in return.

In the present context, the poet has shown the anguish of unrequited love. The knight met a fairy-like beautiful lady in the meadows. Enchanted by this beautiful figure he fell in love with her. But the lady ditched him and hilled him to sleep. Knight then had a dream. He had a vision of kings, princes, and warriors who were pale and looked as if they had starved. They warned him that he had been bewitched by the beautiful lady without mercy. They were also bewitched by the beautiful lady. Then the knight found himself on the cold hillside feeling the death-like cold of his dream. The lady disappeared and forced him to loiter aimlessly with the anguish of unrequited love. She seduced him with her beauty and sensuality and enslaved him. The knight felt alienated and desolated.

6. Who are the opening lines of 'La Belle Dafne Sans Merci' addressed to?

Ans: The knight-at-arms is being addressed at the beginning of the poem.

7. What did the lady give to the knight at Arms?

Ans: The lady gave him relish sweet roots, wild honey, and manna dew i.e. nectar of the gods.

8. Attempt a description of the dream that the knight has in the cave.

Ans: See above Qno. 3 (Answer the following question briefly in your own words.)

9. Whom did the knight meet?

Ans: The Knight met a beautiful lady.

10. And this is why I sojourn here.

Alone and palely loitering.

Though the sedge has wither'd from the Lake

And no birds sing.

Ans: These lines have been taken from the poem 'La Belle Dame Sans Merci' composed by John Keats.

The knight has been bewitched by a beautiful lady who had professed her love, and gave him sweet roots, wild honey, and manna dew. But she was a lady without mercy who vanished without fulfilling the promise of love. The chill has withered the sedge from the lake and no birds are singing. But the knight is forced to loiter all alone, aimlessly with the burden of unrequited love.

11. In 'La Belle Dame Sans Merci', who is it whose granary is full?

Ans: In 'La Belle Dame Sans Merci' the squirrel's granary is full.

12. What did the beautiful lady sing for the knight at arms?

Ans: The beautiful lady sings a faery's song for the knight at arms.

13. What did the beautiful lady give the knight at arms to eat?

Ans: The beautiful lady gives the knight at arms relish sweet roots, wild honey, and manna dew to eat.

14. What did the knight at arms do for the beautiful lady and what did she do for him?

Ans: The knight made a garland for her head, bracelets, and a fragrant zone for her.

She sings a faery's song for him and gives him relish of sweet roots, wild honey, and manna dew to eat.

15. Where did the knight see a lily?

Ans: The knight saw a lily on the face of the lady.

16. What did the lady do in her cave?

Ans: The fair lady took the knight to her fairy cave. In the cave, the lady wept bitterly and sight sorely. Being overwhelmed by her expression of love, the knight kissed her wild and beautiful eyes. Then the lady lulled the knight to sleep.

17. Give the description of the lady the knight met.

Ans: See above Qno. 2(Answer the following question briefly in your own words.)

18. I met a lady in the meads,

Full beautiful-a faery's child,

Her hair was long, her foot was light,

And her eyes were wild.

Ans: These lines have been quoted from the poem,' La Belle Dame Sans Merci' by John Keats.

This stanza continues to describe when the knight met a lady in the meadows who according to him was very beautiful with a face like a fairy's child, her hair was very long and her foot was light. Her eyes have been mentioned as wild. He was so overwhelmed by her beauty. The Knight got attracted to the charm and beauty of the lady and fell in love with her

19. Where did the lady take the knight?

Ans: The lady takes the knight to a fairy cave.

20. What did the knight see in his dream on the hillside?

Ans: See above Qno. 3(Answer the following question briefly in your own words.)

21. What is the appearance of the lady?

Ans: The lady in the poem 'La Belle Dafne Sans Merci' was a beautiful fairy-like lady. She had long hair he lively appearance was apparent in her wild eyes. her movement was also graceful.

22. She found me roots of relish sweet,

And honey wild, and manna-dew,

And sure in language strange, she said

"I love thee true".

Ans: These lines have been quoted from the poem,' La Belle Dame Sans Merci' by John Keats.

This stanza continues to describe the fairy woman's supernatural qualities. She feeds him sweet roots, wild honey, and manna. The "roots of relish sweet" refer to her human qualities, but the manna and the wild honey are symbolic of her supernatural qualities. In the Jewish religion, it is told that God fed the Israelites bread from heaven called manna. This same God promised the Israelites a land flowing with milk and honey. Thus, the fact that the fairy woman was able to feed him bread from heaven, wild honey, and roots suggests that the fairy is part human, part supernatural. The reference to "language strange" is yet another evidence of the lady's unnatural lineage.

Extra-Imp question notes

1. What do the words 'La Belle Dame Sans Merci' mean?

Ans: The words 'La Belle Dame <u>Sans Merci</u>' mean "the beautiful lady without mercy".

2. What is the condition of the knight?

Ans: The Knight was loitering aimlessly with the anguish of unrequited love. He was pale haggard and tired looking. His forehead was sweaty with anguish and fever. He was sick and depressed.

3. What did the lady say to the knight?

Ans: In a strange language she said to the knight "I love thee true".

Some More Questions and Answers

1. How does Keats suggest the season in his ballad?

The season in the poem is late autumn or early winter season. Keats describes this season through dry grass, squirrel's granary, harvest, and absence of birds. The grass on the bank of lake is dry. The squirrel keeps its storage full with grains because if the winter grows, it cannot go out for collecting food. The harvest is also over. No birds sing here because they have moved some other place with favourable climate. Thus Keats describes the season that indirectly points out the unfavourable condition of the knight.

2. Narrate the sad tale of the knight at arms. Describe how the knight fell in love with the beautiful lady and

declared the love and passion for her.

The knight met a beautiful lady in a meadow. He made a garland of flowers and bracelets for her. He put her on his moving horse. She gave him delicious roots, wild honey and the heavenly food manna. She told that she loved him truly. She took him to her cave and wept out of grief. But he kissed her eyes and consoled with his love. She then lulled him to sleep. In the dream, he was warned by dreadful pale kings, princes and warriors about the lady. They told that the beautiful lady had made him a slave mercilessly. He woke up and found him alone on the hill side. Since then, he has been walking aimlessly here.

3. What happened at the elfin grot?

Elfin grot refers to a cave occupied by little angel-like super natural beings called elfs. In Keats' poem, the beautiful lady takes the knight to such a cave. There the lady started weeping out of grief. He kissed her eyes and consoled with his love. She then lulled him to sleep. In the dream, he was warned by dreadful pale kings, princes and warriors about the lady. They told that the beautiful lady had made him a slave mercilessly. This is what happened at the elfin grot. The introduction of such cave, elf and dream element add more charms to medieval theme of the poem. It is also assumed that the lady has already cheated many kings, princes and warriors who appear in the dream.

4. Bring out the ballad features in the poem.

Ballad is a narrative form of poetry. It often begins with a question and the answer comes in the form of story. Keats has written "La Belle Dame Sans Merci" in ballad form. It begins with the question why the knight is so worried and walks alone on this hill side. Then the answer comes in the form of knight's sad story of love affair with a beautiful lady. A ballad is generally rhythmic in four line stanza, second and fourth line rhyming. This poem is also musical and lines end with - Child, wild – long, song- wide, side. Ballad also uses refrain – some lines are repeated. In this poem, for example, the line – "O, what can ail thee, knight-at-arms" is repeated. The poem also uses medieval elements that is common with ballad.

5. Bring out the romantic, medieval and supernatural elements in the poem?

The poem "La Belle Dame Sans Merci" has romantic elements. The story itself is a love story. The knight falls in love with a beautiful lady. Usually lovers will exchange gifts. The knight gives her a garland of flowers and bracelets. The lady also gives him wild honey and manna. The poem is highly romantic when she says, "I love thee true" and he kisses her eyes four times. The story also has medieval elements. Knight is commonly found only in medieval period. Again, in medieval period, people believed in supernatural elements such as ghost and elfs. The lady in the poem appears to be a ghost. She, the elfs and the cave all suddenly disappear. Thus the poem is rich with romantic, medieval and supernatural elements.

A critical appreciation of the poem

According to Brian Stone (The Poetry of Keats) "with its haunting medieval resonances, the poem (-La Belle") is the last of those for which Keats drew on the literature and folk love of the

Middle Ages. Like Blake's "The Sick Rose" the poem raises by powerful images the ideas of love, corruption, and death...The verification and the process of narration by dialogue show Keats to be deeply imbued with the spirit and techniques of the medieval ballad".

The story moves in a circular manner. The speaker meets a Knight in a winter landscape from which the birds have departed, the sedge has withered and where no birds sing. The squirrel's granary is full and the harvest is done. All these details point to the season—it is the end of autumn and winter has arrived. Winter is a season of 'lifelessness' or inactivity.' The Knight's physical appearance synchronizes with the winters desolation.' The speaker is eager to know why the woe-begone pale-looking Knight-at-arms is loitering aimlessly in this bleak landscape. From this desolate setting, the speaker is transported to a 'dream' world of sexual bliss—to the supernatural world. The Knight describes his blissful experience in detail. The lady whom he meets in the mead is a fairy's child with wild, wild eves. He is enamoured of her, offers her gifts, rides with her on his 'pacing steed' she sings fairy songs in strange language and seems to convince him about her genuine love. The lady is presented as eerie being. He rides to her elfin grot, is fed on heavenly delicacies. On 'such choice natural products' as "honey wild and manna dew". 'It is apparent then the plenty is a part of the enchantment', it 'lures him to acts of love and to the ensuing sleep in her arms'. 'With a sudden chill of nightmare,' he sees pale kings, princes and pale warriors—"death pale were they all". With starved lips and parched tongues, they gazed at him as if they warned him that he was "in thrall" of La Belle Dame Sans Merci.

The horrifying description of the kings, princes, and warriors is significant in the poem. The Knight after the erotic bliss finds himself in the realm of death. "The starved lips" has a Shakespearean connotation implying starved to death. Incidentally, the speaker had already observed the signs of sickness and decay in the Knight's appearance. Perhaps he can now, after listening to the Knight's tale, easily surmise that the Knight himself is responsible for his own plight because he 'was active and willing in his own seduction'.

The five fold repetition of pale links the ballad with "As Hermes Once" in considering the act of love in connection with death. The Knight's nightmare can be interpreted in an other way. 'It is as if the Knight was taken beyond life, saw in the hereafter others, who like himself had been seduced by the enchantress and was returned to this world weakened and corrupted, past cure, by his experience.' (Brian Stone).

The poet has used assonances and alliterations. The poem's movement is slow and deliberate since Keats intends the reader to 'experience' and share the experiences of the Knight and the speaker.

The bleak wintry setting suits the temperament and appearance of the Knight, whose existence is meaningless, he is completely cut off from natural and supernatural world, he is 'unprovided' for and is under the spell of the beautiful lady without mercy. The Knight who is supposed to be an adventurer, a protector of law and of people has lost all his powers. He is still the Knight-at-arms, but with a difference, he is aimlessly wandering, he is in 'thrall', a captive.

Some of the images (in the poem) including those of rose and lily are taken from Burton's Anatomy of Melancholy (Refer to the Section on Love—Melancholy). The poem 'haunts the mind of the reader with the music of its particular tragic themes.' "The Knight-at-arms of "La Belle Dame Sans Merci" inhabits his own memorable limbo: possessing neither the joys of the girl nor the finality of death, existing neither in the dream nor in the active life, he is "alone and palely loitering" a haggard figure in a desolate landscape.

****

CHAPTER FIVE

Mac Flecknoe

Mac Flecknoe

BY JOHN DRYDEN

A Satire upon the True-blue Protestant Poet T.S.

All human things are subject to decay,
And, when Fate summons, monarchs must obey:
This Flecknoe found, who, like Augustus, young
Was call'd to empire, and had govern'd long:
In prose and verse, was own'd, without dispute
Through all the realms of Non-sense, absolute.
This aged prince now flourishing in peace,
And blest with issue of a large increase,
Worn out with business, did at length debate
To settle the succession of the State:
And pond'ring which of all his sons was fit
To reign, and wage immortal war with wit;
Cry'd, 'tis resolv'd; for nature pleads that he
Should only rule, who most resembles me:
Shadwell alone my perfect image bears,
Mature in dullness from his tender years.
Shadwell alone, of all my sons, is he
Who stands confirm'd in full stupidity.
The rest to some faint meaning make pretence,
But Shadwell never deviates into sense.

Some beams of wit on other souls may fall,
Strike through and make a lucid interval;
But Shadwell's genuine night admits no ray,
His rising fogs prevail upon the day:
Besides his goodly fabric fills the eye,
And seems design'd for thoughtless majesty:
Thoughtless as monarch oaks, that shade the plain,
And, spread in solemn state, supinely reign.
Heywood and Shirley were but types of thee,
Thou last great prophet of tautology:
Even I, a dunce of more renown than they,
Was sent before but to prepare thy way;
And coarsely clad in Norwich drugget came
To teach the nations in thy greater name.
My warbling lute, the lute I whilom strung
When to King John of Portugal I sung,
Was but the prelude to that glorious day,
When thou on silver Thames did'st cut thy way,
With well tim'd oars before the royal barge,
Swell'd with the pride of thy celestial charge;
And big with hymn, commander of an host,
The like was ne'er in Epsom blankets toss'd.
Methinks I see the new Arion sail,
The lute still trembling underneath thy nail.
At thy well sharpen'd thumb from shore to shore
The treble squeaks for fear, the basses roar:
Echoes from Pissing-Alley, Shadwell call,
And Shadwell they resound from Aston Hall.
About thy boat the little fishes throng,
As at the morning toast, that floats along.
Sometimes as prince of thy harmonious band
Thou wield'st thy papers in thy threshing hand.
St. Andre's feet ne'er kept more equal time,

Not ev'n the feet of thy own Psyche's rhyme:
Though they in number as in sense excel;
So just, so like tautology they fell,
That, pale with envy, Singleton forswore
The lute and sword which he in triumph bore
And vow'd he ne'er would act Villerius more.
Here stopt the good old sire; and wept for joy
In silent raptures of the hopeful boy.
All arguments, but most his plays, persuade,
That for anointed dullness he was made.
Close to the walls which fair Augusta bind,
(The fair Augusta much to fears inclin'd)
An ancient fabric, rais'd t'inform the sight,
There stood of yore, and Barbican it hight:
A watch tower once; but now, so fate ordains,
Of all the pile an empty name remains.
From its old ruins brothel-houses rise,
Scenes of lewd loves, and of polluted joys.
Where their vast courts, the mother-strumpets keep,
And, undisturb'd by watch, in silence sleep.
Near these a nursery erects its head,
Where queens are form'd, and future heroes bred;
Where unfledg'd actors learn to laugh and cry,
Where infant punks their tender voices try,
And little Maximins the gods defy.
Great Fletcher never treads in buskins here,
Nor greater Jonson dares in socks appear;
But gentle Simkin just reception finds
Amidst this monument of vanish'd minds:
Pure clinches, the suburbian muse affords;
And Panton waging harmless war with words.
Here Flecknoe, as a place to fame well known,
Ambitiously design'd his Shadwell's throne.

For ancient Decker prophesi'd long since,
That in this pile should reign a mighty prince,
Born for a scourge of wit, and flail of sense:
To whom true dullness should some Psyches owe,
But worlds of Misers from his pen should flow;
Humorists and hypocrites it should produce,
Whole Raymond families, and tribes of Bruce.
Now Empress Fame had publisht the renown,
Of Shadwell's coronation through the town.
Rous'd by report of fame, the nations meet,
From near Bun-Hill, and distant Watling-street.
No Persian carpets spread th'imperial way,
But scatter'd limbs of mangled poets lay:
From dusty shops neglected authors come,
Martyrs of pies, and reliques of the bum.
Much Heywood, Shirley, Ogleby there lay,
But loads of Shadwell almost chok'd the way.
Bilk'd stationers for yeoman stood prepar'd,
And Herringman was Captain of the Guard.
The hoary prince in majesty appear'd,
High on a throne of his own labours rear'd.
At his right hand our young Ascanius sat
Rome's other hope, and pillar of the state.
His brows thick fogs, instead of glories, grace,
And lambent dullness play'd around his face.
As Hannibal did to the altars come,
Sworn by his sire a mortal foe to Rome;
So Shadwell swore, nor should his vow be vain,
That he till death true dullness would maintain;
And in his father's right, and realm's defence,
Ne'er to have peace with wit, nor truce with sense.
The king himself the sacred unction made,
As king by office, and as priest by trade:

In his sinister hand, instead of ball,
He plac'd a mighty mug of potent ale;
Love's kingdom to his right he did convey,
At once his sceptre and his rule of sway;
Whose righteous lore the prince had practis'd young,
And from whose loins recorded Psyche sprung,
His temples last with poppies were o'er spread,
That nodding seem'd to consecrate his head:
Just at that point of time, if fame not lie,
On his left hand twelve reverend owls did fly.
So Romulus, 'tis sung, by Tiber's brook,
Presage of sway from twice six vultures took.
Th'admiring throng loud acclamations make,
And omens of his future empire take.
The sire then shook the honours of his head,
And from his brows damps of oblivion shed
Full on the filial dullness: long he stood,
Repelling from his breast the raging god;
At length burst out in this prophetic mood:
Heavens bless my son, from Ireland let him reign
To far Barbadoes on the Western main;
Of his dominion may no end be known,
And greater than his father's be his throne.
Beyond love's kingdom let him stretch his pen;
He paus'd, and all the people cry'd Amen.
Then thus, continu'd he, my son advance
Still in new impudence, new ignorance.
Success let other teach, learn thou from me
Pangs without birth, and fruitless industry.
Let Virtuosos in five years be writ;
Yet not one thought accuse thy toil of wit.
Let gentle George in triumph tread the stage,
Make Dorimant betray, and Loveit rage;

Let Cully, Cockwood, Fopling, charm the pit,
And in their folly show the writer's wit.
Yet still thy fools shall stand in thy defence,
And justify their author's want of sense.
Let 'em be all by thy own model made
Of dullness, and desire no foreign aid:
That they to future ages may be known,
Not copies drawn, but issue of thy own.
Nay let thy men of wit too be the same,
All full of thee, and differing but in name;
But let no alien Sedley interpose
To lard with wit thy hungry Epsom prose.
And when false flowers of rhetoric thou would'st cull,
Trust Nature, do not labour to be dull;
But write thy best, and top; and in each line,
Sir Formal's oratory will be thine.
Sir Formal, though unsought, attends thy quill,
And does thy Northern Dedications fill.
Nor let false friends seduce thy mind to fame,
By arrogating Jonson's hostile name.
Let Father Flecknoe fire thy mind with praise,
And Uncle Ogleby thy envy raise.
Thou art my blood, where Jonson has no part;
What share have we in Nature or in Art?
Where did his wit on learning fix a brand,
And rail at arts he did not understand?
Where made he love in Prince Nicander's vein,
Or swept the dust in Psyche's humble strain?
Where sold he bargains, whip-stitch, kiss my arse,
Promis'd a play and dwindled to a farce?
When did his muse from Fletcher scenes purloin,
As thou whole Eth'ridge dost transfuse to thine?
But so transfus'd as oil on waters flow,

His always floats above, thine sinks below.
This is thy province, this thy wondrous way,
New humours to invent for each new play:
This is that boasted bias of thy mind,
By which one way, to dullness, 'tis inclin'd,
Which makes thy writings lean on one side still,
And in all changes that way bends thy will.
Nor let thy mountain belly make pretence
Of likeness; thine's a tympany of sense.
A tun of man in thy large bulk is writ,
But sure thou 'rt but a kilderkin of wit.
Like mine thy gentle numbers feebly creep,
Thy Tragic Muse gives smiles, thy Comic sleep.
With whate'er gall thou sett'st thy self to write,
Thy inoffensive satires never bite.
In thy felonious heart, though venom lies,
It does but touch thy Irish pen, and dies.
Thy genius calls thee not to purchase fame
In keen iambics, but mild anagram:
Leave writing plays, and choose for thy command
Some peaceful province in acrostic land.
There thou may'st wings display and altars raise,
And torture one poor word ten thousand ways.
Or if thou would'st thy diff'rent talents suit,
Set thy own songs, and sing them to thy lute.
He said, but his last words were scarcely heard,
For Bruce and Longvil had a trap prepar'd,
And down they sent the yet declaiming bard.
Sinking he left his drugget robe behind,
Born upwards by a subterranean wind.
The mantle fell to the young prophet's part,
With double portion of his father's art.

Restoration Age's social, political, historical and literary tendencies

The Restoration Age (1660-1700) is a significant period in English history and literature. It began when Charles II was restored to the English throne after the Puritan Commonwealth under Oliver Cromwell. This era saw the revival of monarchy, new political changes, and flourishing art and literature. Contemporary texts reflect the social, historical, political, and literary trends of the time.

❑ **Social Tendencies**: Here are the social tendencies of the Restoration period:

Return of Aristocratic Life: The aristocracy regained prestige after the strict Puritan rule. Court life under Charles II became lavish, focusing on luxury, fashion, and indulgence.

Moral Looseness: Society embraced a more relaxed approach to morality, especially among the upper class. Libertinism, or the pursuit of pleasure without moral restraint, became popular. It is seen in William Wycherley's "The Country Wife" (1675), which satirized loose morals.

Revival of Entertainment and Theatres: Theatres, which were closed during the Puritan era, reopened. Comedy of Manners plays became popular, making fun of the upper class's behavior and vanity.

Rise of the Middle Class: The growing importance of trade and commerce led to the rise of the middle class. Merchants and professionals started gaining influence. By this, the middle class challenged aristocratic dominance.

Urbanization and Social Interaction: Cities, especially London, expanded. Coffeehouses became popular places for intellectual and political discussions and served as hubs for social interaction.

❏ **Political Tendencies**: Chronologically, political tendencies are given below:

English Civil War (1642-1651): The war between the Royalists and Parliamentarians ended with Charles I's execution. Oliver Cromwell took control and led the republic.

Commonwealth and Cromwell's (1649-1660) Rule: Cromwell ruled as Lord Protector with strict Puritan laws banning entertainment. His harsh rule made people want the monarchy back.

Restoration of the Monarchy (1660): In 1660, Charles II returned as king. He worked with Parliament to avoid absolute power. John Dryden wrote,

Beware the fury of a patient man,
It shows the tension between the king and the people.

Exclusion Crisis (1679-1681): Religion caused conflict. The Whigs wanted to exclude James II (a Catholic) from the throne, while the Tories supported him. Dryden said in "Absalom and Achitophel" (1681),

No king could govern, nor no God could please.
It shows the instability.

Glorious Revolution (1688): James II was overthrown. William and Mary took the throne and led to a constitutional monarchy. John Milton's "Paradise Lost" (1667) captured this desire for freedom with Satan's quote,

Better to reign in Hell than serve in Heaven.

It represents the human desire for autonomy, a key idea during this political change.

❏ **Literary Features/Tendencies**: Restoration literature reflects the complexity of its age. Sundry features are given below:

Satire and Political Allegory: Writers like John Dryden used satire to address political issues. In "Absalom and Achitophel," Dryden uses biblical figures to represent real-life politicians with humor.

Of these the false Achitophel was first;

....

For close designs and crooked counsels fit,
Sagacious, bold, and turbulent of wit.

Comedy of Manners: Plays like "The Way of the World" by William Congreve and "The Country Wife" (1675) by William Wycherley focus on the behavior of the elite by mocking their vanity and hypocrisy. Wycherley uses characters like Horner, who pretends to be impotent to seduce women, to satirize the immorality of the upper class.

Heroic Tragedy: "Oroonoko" (1688) by Aphra Behn combines romance and tragedy. It tells the story of an African prince who is enslaved and betrayed. This reflects the growing interest in individual heroism and the darker side of imperialism.

Religious Themes: John Milton's "Paradise Lost" (1667) was highly influential during the Restoration. Its exploration of free will, sin, and redemption speaks to the moral and religious questions of the time. Milton's portrayal of Satan as a tragic figure shows the shifting attitudes toward authority and rebellion.

Realism: Literature in this period often portrayed human flaws realistically. In "The Way of the World," characters are not idealized heroes but flawed individuals navigating a world of deceit.

Others: Love for classical literature, neglect of lower-class people, and less importance given to nature are also trends of this era.

❏ **Introduction to Restoration**: The term "Restoration" refers to Charles II's return to power in 1660. The king's return brought back the monarchy, the Anglican Church, and the aristocratic way of life. It was also a time of new freedoms and a reaction against the strict Puritan values of the previous era.

❏ **Historical and Political Background of the Restoration Age**: Chronologically, historical and political tendencies are given below:

The English Civil War (1642-1651): England experienced a long and bloody civil war before the Restoration. The battle was fought between the Royalists (supporters of King Charles I) and the Parliamentarians (those who supported Parliament). The war ended in 1649 with the execution of King Charles I, and the monarchy was abolished. England became a republic, but Oliver Cromwell held the real power. He led the Parliamentarian forces to victory.

The Commonwealth and Cromwell's Rule (1649-1660): After Charles I's execution, England was declared a Commonwealth, which meant it was a republic without a king. Oliver Cromwell became the most powerful figure during this time. In 1653, he took the title of Lord Protector and ruled like a military dictator. Cromwell imposed strict Puritan values, banning entertainment like theatres and festivities.

His rule was harsh, and people grew tired of it. When Cromwell died in 1658, his son Richard Cromwell took over. However, he was not a strong leader. This caused political instability, and many people began to miss the monarchy.

The Restoration of the Monarchy (1660): With the country in chaos, Parliament invited Charles II, the son of Charles I, back from exile in France. In 1660, Charles II was restored to the throne, starting the Restoration period. People celebrated because they were tired of the strict Puritan rule. Theatres were reopened, and culture and entertainment returned.

However, Charles II was careful to avoid repeating his father's mistakes. He balanced his power with Parliament. He understood that people would not accept an absolute monarchy again. As John Dryden wrote in "Absalom and Achitophel" (1681),

Beware the fury of a patient man.

This quote reflects the tension between the king and the people. Here, both had to proceed cautiously to avoid conflict.

Political Tensions and the Exclusion Crisis (1679-1681): Religion became a major political issue during the Restoration. Charles II was Protestant, but his brother James, who was next in line for the throne, was Catholic. This worried many Protestants, and the Exclusion Crisis began. Many members of Parliament tried to pass a law to prevent James from becoming king.

This conflict led to the rise of England's first political parties: the Whigs and the Tories. The Whigs wanted to exclude James, and the Tories supported the traditional line of succession. Although the Exclusion Bill failed, it showed Parliament's growing power. This political environment influenced literature, such as In "Absalom and Achitophel," Dryden shows how the masses are easily swayed and unreliable. Dryden says about them,

No king could govern, nor no God could please.

The Glorious Revolution (1688): When Charles II died in 1685, his Catholic brother James II became king. However, James's attempts to promote Catholicism caused unrest. In 1688, James II was overthrown in what became known as the Glorious Revolution. William of Orange and his wife Mary (James's Protestant daughter) were invited to take the throne. This marked the end of political instability during the Restoration period.

The Glorious Revolution led to the creation of a constitutional monarchy, where laws and Parliament limited the king's power and gained more authority. This event helped shape modern British democracy. Literature of the time reflected these changes, such as John Milton's "Paradise Lost" (1667), which explored themes of rebellion and the desire for freedom. In the poem, Satan says,

Better to reign in Hell than serve in Heaven.

It represents the human desire for autonomy, a key idea during this political change.

In conclusion, the Restoration Age was a rich period of political change and literary innovation. It blended old traditions with new ideas, especially in the realms of satire, comedy, and tragedy. The writers captured the complexities of their society, commenting on politics, morality, and human behavior in ways that still resonate today.

An Introduction to MacFlecknoe

About the poem

MacFleknoe is a mock-heroic poem.

"Mock-heroic or mock-epic works are typically satires or parodies that mock common Classical stereotypes of heroes and heroic literature. Typically, mock-heroic works either put a fool in the role of the hero or exaggerate the heroic qualities to such a point that they become absurd."(Wikipedia)

Background of the poem

Dryden's intention in writing "Mac Flecknoe" was to expose Shadwell as an inferior writer. Dryden parodies Shadwell cruelly, in spite of the fact that he maintains a strategic distance from mockery. Rather, Dryden uses the outstanding ability of his wit, extremely sharp, to expose Shadwell's writing as uninteresting and boring. Early in the poem, Dryden uses hyperbole or overstatement to pressure the duskiness of Shadwell's creative ability and imagination.

Points to remember

Dryden and Shadwell

John Dryden wrote "Mac Flecknoe" to satirize another English writer, Thomas Shadwell. Dryden and Shadwell had once treated each other amicably but became enemies because of their differing views on the following:

Politics - Dryden was a Tory; Shadwell was a Whig.

Religion - Shadwell offended Dryden when he ridiculed Catholic and Anglican clerics in his play The Lancashire-Witches, and Teague o Divelly the Irish-Priest (1682). Dryden was thinking about turning into a Catholic at the time (1686).

Different Opinion - Dryden and Shadwell varied strongly on who was the better essayist: Shakespeare or Ben Jonson. Dryden took the piece of Shakespeare; Shadwell adored Jonson.

Richard Flecknoe

Richard Flecknoe (1600-1678) was an English dramatist and poet whose writing was parodied by Dryden. In "Mac Flecknoe," Dryden depicts him as the King of Nonsense and Shadwell as the son of the King of Nonsense. Shadwell assumes the crown as Mac Flecknoe. (Mac means son of.)

Summary of Mac Flecknoe
L 1-29

In the poem, the poet (Dryden) uses the third-person perspective and Thomas Shadwell is introduced as "A Satire on the True-blue Protestant T.S."

Dryden introduces Flecknoe, who, compared to the Roman Emperor Augustus, was called to the throne when he was young. He rules the Kingdom of Nonsense peacefully at this time. But he is growing old enough and he wants to choose the next king of his state.

Flecknoe thinks about which of his sons is perfect for the throne. It will be the man who looks like him most. In this respect, Shadwell, who is mature in dullness from his childhood, is a perfect successor. He is "confirm'd in full stupidity" (line 18). While some of his have some sense, he never has any sense whatsoever Shadwell's "genuine night admits no ray" (line 23).

L 30-64

Flecknoe believes Shadwell "the last great prophet of tautology" (line 30), parallel to Heywood and Shirley before him. Truly, Flecknoe was a prestigious dull, however, he was only a harbinger, a precursor, to set up the route for a definitive dullard, his son. Infamous authors who preceded Shadwell periodically showed the dimmest shine of wit but Shadwell never composed a line that seemed well and good.

When Mac Flecknoe's majestic barge advances on the River Thames for the first time, people gather to yell his name and "the little fishes throng" (line 49) around his vessel. His elderly father "wept for joy / In silent raptures of the hopeful boy" (L 60-61). Nobody can disagree against Shadwell as the perfect King of Nonsense, for the greater part of his works—specifically his plays—specify "that for anointed dullness he was made" (line 63).

L 65-94

Shadwell takes the position of royalty in a district of Augusta (London) where "brothel-houses rise" (line 7). Close-by is a nursery for kids who will be trained as performers. The plays of Fletcher and Jonson (John Fletcher and Ben Jonson) are never staged in this place, however, the dull and inferior plays of Shadwell were staged here.

L 95-134

Empress Fame publishes the account of Shadwell's name. Citizens hearing him meets together. There are no Persian carpets lining the road, only "scatter'd limbs of mangled poets" (line 99). Writers like Heywood, Shirley, and Ogleby lay in the road, but yet it is, for the most part, Shadwell that stops up it.

Finally, the prince shows up in all his magnificence, sitting on a throne. Flecknoe compares Shadwell to Ascanius, son of Aeneas, who sat at his father's right hand and inherited the kingdom. Shadwell's eyebrows are like thick fogs, and dullness twirls about his appearance.

Shadwell swears he will keep up dullness until his death. He will never show wit and sign a true sense.

The king places a mug of ale in his son's hand. While holding a mug of ale in his left hand, Shadwell holds the composition of his play Love's Kingdom in his right, announcing it "his sceptre and his rule of sway" (line 123). At that moment from his left hand fly twelve owls, an occurrence that reminds the observers of Romulus, legendary co-founder of ancient Rome. Twelve vultures proclaimed his rule.

The admiring crowd yells for all happening.

L 135-164

Flecknoe shakes his dewy forehead and scatters the drops on his son. He stands in a prophetic state of mind and announces that Heaven should bless his son and he shall rule from Ireland to Barbados; there will be no end to his conclusion to his territory and it will be more prominent than his father's.

Flecknoe stops to let the people cry "Amen!" He proclaims that his son still advances in impudence and stupid.. Others can learn achievement, but from Flecknoe, Shadwell has learned "pangs without birth, and fruitless industry" (line 148).

L 165-217

Flecknoe expresses the expectation that his son "advance in new impudence, new ignorance" (line 146) and compose virtuosic plays showing no confirmation of knowledge. Also, he says, let other essayists copy his son. The main distinction amongst Shadwell and them, he says, will be their names. Flecknoe advises his son to avoid stressing to choose "false flowers of rhetoric" (line 165). Rather, he need only confide his common senses, and dullness will pour forward. For motivation, Shadwell should copy his father rather than writers of wit, like Ben Jonson.

While still speaking Flecknoe suddenly vanishes through a trap door. A wind carries his majestic robe upward, and it falls upon the shoulders of the new King of Nonsense—Shadwell, Mac Flecknoe.

Mac Flecknoe Quotes and Analysis

1.All human things are subject to decay,
   And, when Fate summons, monarchs must obey:
   This Flecknoe found, who, like Augustus, young

Was call'd to Empire, and had govern'd long:
In Prose and Verse, was own'd, without dispute
Through all the Realms of Non-sense, absolute.
Mac Flecknoe, lines 1-6

In these first lines, Dryden clearly establishes his satiric voice. He is using grand language, tone, ideas, and historical allusion to discuss the leader of the realm of Nonsense, assuredly not the name readers were expecting. Comparisons to Rome, the evocation of such universal themes such as death and fate, and the use of heroic couplets serve to discomfit and amuse the reader when they start to realize what Dryden is up to. In the lines that follow, Dryden skewers Shadwell in the harshest of ways, but nowhere is the tone bitter or the insults blatant. Rather, through this mock-heroic style, Dryden suggests just how lacking in merit his subject is.

2.And pond'ring which of all his Sons was fit
To Reign, and wage immortal War with Wit;
Cry'd, 'tis resolv'd; for Nature pleads that he
Should only rule, who most resembles me:
Sh—— alone my perfect image bears,
Mature in dullness from his tender years.
Mac Flecknoe, lines 11-16

Flecknoe uses an encomiastic tone to introduce his son, a man who wages war with wit and has been dull practically since he was born. This is tremendously ironic, of course, and Dryden heaps on the insults by spelling Shadwell's name as "Sh--," a stand-in for "shit" if there ever was one. He will continue to evoke shit throughout the poem; critic Virginia Brackett argues that lines 49-50 ("About thy boat little fishes throng, / As at the morning toast, that floats along") are an allusion to "sewage floating on top of the water." During the procession, "loads of Sh-- almost chok'd the way" (line 103). There is very little ambiguity about it - Dryden is saying that Shadwell and his work are no better than excrement.

3.Close to the Walls which fair Augusta bind,
(The fair Augusta much to fears inclin'd)
An ancient fabrick, rais'd t' inform the sight,
There stood of yore, and Barbican it hight:
A watch Tower once; but now, so Fate ordains,
Of all the Pile an empty name remains.
From its old Ruins Brothel-houses rise,
Scenes of lewd loves, and of polluted joys.
Where their vast Courts, the Mother-Strumpets keep,
And, undisturb'd by Watch, in silence sleep.
Near these a Nursery erects its head,
Where Queens are form'd, and future Hero's bred;
Where unfledg'd Actors learn to laugh and cry,
Where infant Punks their tender Voices try,
And little Maximins the Gods defy.
Mac Flecknoe, lines 64-78

It is absolutely no accident that Shadwell's glorious coronation takes place in a neighborhood such as this. The Roman edifices are now in ruins, suggesting that English arts are in ruins as well. The denizens of the neighborhood primarily include prostitutes and "unfledg'd actors" and "infant punks." Love is "lewd" and joy "polluted" (line 71). A few lines later Dryden adds that only clowns (Simkin) find "just reception" (line 81) and that it is a "monument to vanish'd minds" (line 82). The term "Maximins" refers to the inhabitants of Augusta, but ironically the Latin meaning of "greatness" does not apply. All is empty, vile, and ignoble. The past is glorious and the present debased.

4.Now Empress Fame had publisht the renown,
Of Sh——'s coronation through the town.

Rous'd by report of fame, the nations meet,
From near Bun-Hill, and distant Watling-street.
No Persian Carpets spread th'imperial way,
But scatter'd limbs of mangled poets lay:
From dusty shops neglected authors come,
Martyrs of Pies, and Reliques of the Bum
Much Heywood, Shirly, Ogleby there lay,
But loads of Sh—— almost choakt the way.
Mac Flecknoe, lines 94-103

This passage absolutely drips with irony. The "Empress Fame" proclaims Shadwell's coronation and nations meet together to rejoice, which of course is a ludicrous thing to imagine given what we know of the corpulent and crass Shadwell. Dryden contrasts this grand image with scatological references and a disturbing image of the severed limbs of other poets (although the "limbs" are actually book pages, it still disturbs). The "martyrs of pies" refers to bakers' use of book pages underneath pies, and "reliques of the bum" refers to book pages being used as toilet paper. Thus, Shadwell's writings are ideally used for nothing better than wiping one's ass and lining the bottom of a street food.

5.At his right hand our young Ascanius sat
Rome's other hope, and pillar of the State.
His Brows thick fogs, instead of glories, grace,
And lambent dullness plaid arround his face.
As Hannibal did to the Altars come,
Sworn by his Syre a mortal Foe to Rome;
So Sh—— swore, nor should his Vow bee vain,
That he till Death true dullness would maintain;
And in his father's Right, and Realms defence,
Ne'er to have peace with Wit, nor truce with Sense.
Mac Flecknoe, lines 108-117

One of Dryden's favored techniques to lampoon Shadwell is to place him in the historical shadow of Rome and its heroes, which, of course, highlights just how far removed from these luminaries Shadwell truly is. Here he suggests that Shadwell is like Ascansius, the son of Aeneas and the founder of the city of Alba Longa. Clearly, Flecknoe is no Aeneas and Shadwell is no Ascansius. When one imagines a Roman hero, one thinks of an aquiline nose, a strong brow and set chin, and intelligent eyes. Here, Shadwell has "thick fogs" about his brow, and his face is filled with "lambent dullness."

Long Questions and Answers

1.Mac Flecknoe As Mock-Epic poem

Mock-epic is a genre of poetry which creates parody by comparing heroic poetry or classical heroes with the fool or poet's target on which he wishes to satirize. Mock-epic doesn't involve the seriousness of the epic. It works as a best way to make great satire because when there is comparison between a minor and the epic object, it results in incongruity and makes the minor object more inferiorizing and funny.

John Dryden's Mac Flecknoe is considered one of the best mock-epic poems of English literature. In it, Dryden attacks his rival and former friend Thomas Shadwell. The following features prove Mac Flecknoe as a Mock-Epic or Mock Heroic :-

• Use of Heroic Couplet – Throughout the poem, Dryden used Heroic couplet (a pair of rhyming lines written in iambic pentameter) . It is commonly used in epic but here the subject of the poem is not of heroic doings of warriors but simply the description of foolishness and dullness of his contemporary rival Shadwell.

• Diction – The diction of the poem is sublime and refined words are used in it but they create opposite effect of inferiorizing Shadwell and Flecknoe. No vulgar words are used in it. This tells us that Dryden was the master of words, he didn't have to use abusive words to make fun of his rival, he did it with respective words. The opening lines glimpse us of an epic but it is the sixth line which describes its mock-epic attribute.

Through all the realms of Nonsense absolute

• Attack with Politeness – Throughout the poem, Dryden makes an incisive attack on his rival but in a polite manner. He used royal words in the poem such as succession, coronation, state, prince, Augustus, empire. Irony is created in his achievements to create satire. His coronation should make him proud but it degrades his status as he was chosen as perfect heir to kingdom of nonsense

Mature in dullness from his tender years

To reign and wage immortal war with wit

• Inflation-Deflation - In mock heroic, the target is first inflated through grand description and high flown words and then deflates him to the ground to create satire. Dryden proudly announces Shadwell's coronation and called him heir but later it was known that he was heir to the kingdom of nonsense. With this treatment, he lost all the uplifting characteristics and thrown back to the ground.

• Comparison with Epic heroes – The deflation of Flecknoe and Shadwell is achieved by their comparison with classical heroes such as :-

Augustus – He was the ruler of Rome succeeding Julius Caesar who ruled over Rome over 40 years. In the poem, Flecknoe was compared to Augustus just like he ruled the empire for a long period since his youth, Flecknoe too ruled the kingdom of Nonsense for a similar period.

Arion – He was a Greek Musician who was kidnapped by pirates and he rescued the situation by inventing a musical note to hypnotise dolphins who sailed him away from pirates. Similarly Shadwell can get only to small fishes while he was crossing Thames River in a barge.

Ascanius – He was a legendary king and hope of Rome. Shadwell is compared to him because just like him he was the hope of a kingdom of nonsense.

Hannibal – He was a military commander of Carthage who in his childhood made promises that until his death he wouldn't be a friend of Rome. Similarly, Shadwell swore from his early age to wage endless war on wit and maintain his dullness.

Romulus – He saw twelve vultures which he perceived as a sign of omen for his future empire, Shadwell too saw owls which was perceived as the coming of age of Shadwell.

Dryden also made allusions to great literary figures such as Jonson, Dekker, Fletcher and Sedley.

• Pretention – The poem is pretended to be the subject of heroic and make reference to great people but in reality the effect of the poem is opposite.

• Degraded setting of coronation – The coronation of Shadwell also reflects the mock heroic theme. His coronation is set in Augusta (London) which is populated by ruins, ill-famed people and brothels. In these brothels, people experienced filthy sexual pleasure and prostitutes sleep undisturbed by watchmen. Near the brothel, there is a school for small children who are getting training to become future heroes and queens. They are taught to cry and defy gods. Degraded poets ruled this place. With the spreading of news about Shadwell coronation, people started gathering in streets and instead of covering paths with Persian carpets, they are decorated with torn works of worthless poets. Unskilled writers including Heywood, Shirley and Ogleby gathered at Shadwell's coronation. Broke book publishers are waiting for him to give him Guard of Honour and Herringman (Publisher of Shadwell) is the captain of them. Along with old Flecknoe, Shadwell appeared in the royal state. Instead of having a bright face and halo surrounding head like a holy figure, fog covered his forehead and dullness was expressed on his face. He swore like Hannibal ,who swore to be enemy with Rome until his death, he too till death maintained his true dullness and took his father's legacy to greater heights and he would never adopt wit and remain senseless forever.

• Comic Ending - At last when Flecknoe was delivering his speech, two characters in Shadwell's The Virtuoso prepare a trap for Flecknoe and he disappeared, leaving his robe and with wind the robe fell on the double times more gifted, the true master of Dullness, Shadwell who would show more nonsense and extend his kingdom of dullness.

Q.Mac Flecknoe as a Lampoon

A personal satire or lampoon is an attack on a particular rival and is usually not accompanied by any reformative zeal. Mac Flecknoe originated in personal malice. It is a retaliatory attack of Thomas Shadwell for having written The Medal of John Bays which in turn was a reply to Dryden's The Medal. Thomas Shadwell's satire was a personal attack on Dryden and an abusive one. Dryden could not pocket the insult meekly; so he wrote Mac Flecknoe as a stinging reply.

While we read Mac Flecknoe we realize that Dryden has no desire to reform Shadwell. As a satire, the poem contains much personal slander, a great deal of which is undeserved by Shadwell. Though not a great writer, Shadwell was not an absolute dunce as made out by Dryden. A remarkable handling of the mock-heroic technique, however reduces Shadwell to a dullard. Throughout the poem, we come across words like 'sense', 'art', 'tautology' 'nature' and 'nonsense'- words often used by Dryden in his prolonged critical warfare with Shadwell.

With consummate skill, Dryden dresses up Shadwell in a heroic armour only in order to reduce him to the size of a pigmy. Flecknoe's part in the poem is simply representative and the main satire is directed against Shadwell 'who stands confirmed in full stupidity'. Dryden calls him the dullest son of Flecknoe.

Shadwell was a born enemy of wit, sense and intelligence. As a dramatist too, Shadwell is a grand failure. His tragedies make one laugh and his comedies induce sleep. He is also ridiculed for his presumptuous imitation of Ben Jonson. All these things fully illustrate that Mac Flacknoe is a personal satire.

However, we are to remember that Dryden's impulses were not merely personal but had a wider scope. He did not merely intend to attack Shadwell, but through him, all the bad poets of his day. Thus certain impersonal impulses also enter the poem giving it a universal dimension. Tautology and bombast are not only to be attacked in Shadwell, but in all other poets who made use of them.

To sum up, in Mac Flecknoe, we have a great deal of personal satire, although much of it is unfair. In fact, much of its pungency, its personal attack is redeemed by its humour and we would like to look upon Shadwell as a great comic creation.

****

Gitanjali (NO. 50)

Gitanjali (NO. 50)
Rabindranath Tagore
I had gone a-begging from door to door in the village
path,
when thy golden chariot appeared in the
distance
like a gorgeous dream and I wondered
who was this King of all kings!
My hopes rose high and methought
my evil days were at an end,
and I stood waiting for alms to be given unasked
and for wealth scattered on all sides in the dust.
The chariot stopped where I stood.
Thy glance fell on me
and thou camest down with a smile.
I felt that the luck of my life had come at last.
Then of a sudden thou didst hold out thy right hand
and say `What hast thou to give to me?'
Ah, what a kingly jest was it
to open thy palm to a beggar to beg!
I was confused and stood undecided,
and then from my wallet I slowly took out
the least little grain of corn

and gave it to thee.
But how great my surprise when at the day's end
I emptied my bag on the floor to find
a least little gram of gold among the poor heap.
I bitterly wept and wished
that I had had the heart to give thee my all.

Annotations

A-begging: the act of begging. Gorgeous: majestic. Alms: money, or anything given in charity. Wallet: the bag in which beggars collect their alms.

Through a parable Rabindrnath Tagore's Gitanjali (NO. 50) conveys to us an idea of the value of charity, love and sacrifice- a spiritual message. God, disguised as a raj beggar, asked for alms from the poet beggar who had himself been going about, asking for alms because he himself had felt the pangs of poverty. Being in no position to give any alms, the poet beggar produced a single grain of corn from his alms bag and gave it to the king of kings. On going home, the poet beggar felt amazed to find a piece of gold in his bag.

The beggar referred to in the poem, _Gitanjali (NO.50)_ is none but the poet himself as well as everyman. One day he was begging from door to door in the village path or it might be the endless wondering of humanity in the wasteland of modernity where there is no hope, no love or no sympathy. En route something unusual happened. There appeared at a distance a golden chariot that made everything bright with its golden hues. The chariot seemed to the poet to be a gorgeous dream —dream of pomp and splendour. The poet thought in wonder who this king of kings was. The "king of kings" referred to in the poem is God, who is the supreme ruler of the universe.

Seeing the golden chariot, the poet became hopeful. His hopes rose limping high. He thought that the king of all kings would give him unlimited wealth as alms and the days of his misery would come to an end. So he stood waiting with eager expectations for the chariot to come near him and for plenty of precious alms to be scattered in the dust.

The chariot came and stopped where the poet stood waiting for the king of kings to come and give him alms. The king's glance fell on him and he came down from the chariot with a smile. The poet now felt that the luck of his life had come at last.

He eagerly hoped for better days in his life. But what happened was not only surprising but contrary to what he had so long hoped for. All on a sudden the king of kings held out his right hand and begged alms of him. The poet was not at all prepared for this unusual behaviour of the king. He was expecting wealth from the king; but instead of fulfilling his hope, the king asked him for alms. The poet thought that the king of kings was simply joking with him. Otherwise, how could the king of kings open his palm to a beggar to beg? In fact, he is the raj beggar in this waste land where he earnestly solicit love, compassion and faith from his fellow subjects, human being. But the world is stuck in the mud of materialism, and spiritualism is altogether missing. However, the poet beggar was utterly confused and stood undecided. After a while he came back to his senses from his confused state of mind. He slowly took out from his wallet the least little grain of corn and gave it to the king of kings. The word 'slowly' used in the poem suggests the poet's reluctance to give alms to the king. It also reveals his miserliness. Again, the expression "least little grain" shows how miserly the poet beggar was.

At the day's end the poet-beggar returned home and emptied his bag on the floor to see what he had collected on that day. His surprise knew no bounds when he found that there was a little grain of gold among the poor heap of alms. He now understood that the king of kings was God Himself and the little piece of gold was given by him. He also understood that this gold had great spiritual value, because it was an embodiment of God's blessing on him. The poet bitterly wept because he gave the king of kings only a little grain of corn. He realized that if he gave Him his all, he would receive much more. He thus lost a great opportunity to surrender himself to God or the lord of life ; and by doing this he could be elevated to a higher spiritual plane from a lower material one. So he said with great regret "I had had the heart to give thee my all." He then realized that the beggar was no other than God Himself in disguise. Thus the poet beggar had been rewarded by God for the act of charity which the poet had done despite his own materialistic penury. In a nutshell, it is an interesting poem which tells a neat little story conveying a precious spiritual message.

Summary of the poem :

One day the beggar-poet was wandering from door to door in a village path collecting alms as usual. All of a sudden, a golden chariot came to his view at some distance like a 'gorgeous dream' and the mendicant wondered that 'King of all kings' must be inside the chariot. Culmination of the beggar's hope was quite natural and he thought that his evil days, the days of penury and uncertainty, must end from that moment. He stood waiting for charity that would be given to him unasked and also expected that such an opulent person must scatter wealth on all sides of the path for the have-nots.

The golden chariot stopped before the mendicant. With a captivating glance and fascinating smile the owner of the chariot got down with pleasant steps and approached to the beggar-poet who started thinking that it was the last moment of catching good luck. At such ecstatic moment the royal owner held out his right hand to the beggar saying "What hast thou to give to me?" The beggar-poet thought that It was nothing but a 'kingly jest' ; otherwise, the royal owner could not beg from a beggar. The beggar was at a loss and stood still doing nothing for a few moments but he had to respond. unenthusiastically the beggar took a little grain of corn from his wallet and handed it to the royal beggar. Thus ended the uneventful day in an ironic way.

At the day's end a great surprise was waiting for the beggar-poet. When he emptied his wallet on the floor to measure the day's collection, he became flabbergasted as a 'grain of gold' was sparkling in his poor collection. He realized that the 'grain of corn' returned as the 'grain of gold' in his alms. The mendicant wept bitterly and then wished that he should have had a mind to give his all to the royal beggar.

Analytical Study Of the poem : The poem No. 50 of Gitanjali is an allegorical poem which contains a surprising story of a beggar told in an interesting way. It is not merely the story of an unknown beggar, it is the story of every man who has to face the puzzling situation in life like the beggar-poet of this poem. The beggar symbolizes human being who is miserly by nature. The miser man only wants and wants, he is not ready to give anything. If the occasion compels him to give anything, he gives the least little part of his wealth reluctantly. Sometimes man has to undergo some ordeal or acid test which he can not realize. God, our supreme father, sometimes appears in earthly shape to test us, to test our humane properties. Human beings, the source of all supreme values, the mine of all sublime qualities, are gradually corrupted in this world with many a subhuman nature, the seven deadly sins of this world. Naturally, in almost all cases man fails to go through the divine trial. For his selfish and covetous nature, man loses heavenly gift and the grace of God. God's revelation is not uncommon and we have to confront God's test any time unexpectedly like the beggar of this poem.

The king of all kings, God himself, is a universal and eternal giver. He gives us everything to make our life happy, comfortable and meaningful. Sometimes God suddenly seeks something from man. Being the owner of all wealth of this world God demands no wealth or money from us. What he seeks from us are love and devotion, our total surrender to him. When we offer anything to God earnestly, God makes no late to return it making thousandfold like the grain of little gold in the poor collection of the mendicant. If we show our close-fisted nature to God, if we deal with him in material value, if we lack spirituality, we have to weep bitterly like the beggar-poet. In this poem, we find the story of a beggar and the story of mankind behind it. There is an apparent meaning and other deep meaning is found beneath the literal one. For this feature this is obviously an allegorical poem.

Deep philosophical meaning of this poem can not be ruled out. One day's incident of the beggar's life may be equated to the purport of the whole life of a man. The beggar's experience cautions us so that we can lead our life scrupulously and judiciously. We have to pay for everything in our life, we can not avoid 'Karma'. Like the beggar's day, man starts his life quite normally. Uncertainty, confusion, indecision, bewilderment, amazement and other deciding factors come before a man. Like the beggar man has to take many decisions in his life. If man becomes confused and stands undecided like the helpless beggar at the ultimate moment and makes some blunder, he has to weep in his old days, no second chance for rectification and amendment comes in this life. In C.G.Rossetti's word "Of labour you shall find the sum." (Uphill). One is rewarded in life as per one's activities. This philosophy of human life is soaked with religious values and ideas. So, this is a religious poem also.

This poem is full of ethical values and the subject matter is like an anecdote. Beside allegorical aspect one does not miss some metaphorical sides of this poem. Climax and anti-climax are present in the narration. The poem is spoken in first person 'I' in a prose narrative style. There is no rhyme and no rhyme scheme but poetic rhythm is there to give it a verse level.

Some Short Questions and Answers

Q 1. "...when thy golden chariot appeared in the distance like a gorgeous dream"- Explain the simile

Dream is something which is unbelievable.Here in the context of the poem, the beggar was begging from one door to another for alms and suddenly he noticed a golden chariot in the distance.So this sight seems nothing short of dreamto the beggar.

Q.2."Ah, what a kingly jest was it..."Who said this and when ?

The mysterious person coming from a golden chariot said this to the poet (beggar).

The poet was shocked and thought it was a royal joke-that a donor is opening His palm in front of a beggar. Here the poet is unaware of the aim behind the king's act of begging. God was testing his charity. The poet was bewildered and confused, but he gave Him a grain of corn from his wallet. At the end of the day, when the poet emptied his bag on the floor, great was his surprise to see a small piece of gold among the grains in the heap. He wept bitterly and regretted that he did not give his all to God.

Q.3. " I bitterly wept and wished that I had had the heart to give thee my all."-Why did the speaker feel so and when ?

Here the speaker is the beggar -poet.He as begging from door to door for alms.But suddenly he saw a golden chariot in the distance and it stopped just in front of the beggar and one person came out of that .Then he asked the beggar "'What hast thou to give to me?'

The poet was shocked and thought it was a royal joke-that a donor is opening His palm in front of a beggar. Here the poet is unaware of the aim behind the king's act of begging. God was testing his charity. The poet was bewildered and confused, but he gave Him a grain of corn from his wallet. At the end of the day, when the poet emptied his bag on the floor, great was his surprise to see a small piece of gold among the grains in the heap. He wept bitterly for not sharing whatever he had inside his bag with the mysterious person.

Q.4.Who is the mysterious person coming from the golden chariot?

The identity of the mysterious person, coming from the golden chariot is not disclosed in the poem directly though many hints are given.From the hints we can decipher it's Almighty God.

Long Questions and Answers

Q.What is the core idea of the poem ?

The lyric is a poetic version of Indian values. Tagore, being Indian has in his mind the virtues of charity, humbleness and sacrifice. The theme of poem is that you get by one hand if you give by other. Unaware of the truth, the poor poet gives a single grain of corn from the heap and later repents if he had the generosity to give everything to God.

The renunciation of all possession is the only way that leads to God. This is the inevitable truth. This lyric of Tagore reminds the Indian epics where God comes in different disguises to test the bounty of their devotees. The generosity of Karna, the love of Krishna for His devotee and poor friend Sudama. The offerings of Sudama in the form of rice turned his poverty to wealth. The generosity, pure love and charity wins the Almighty God and He comes down to help the poor humble lovers of Him.

The style and verse are as simple as other lyrics of Tagore. The simplicity of words, theme and diction maintains the human interest. The form of lyric in a parable is again laudable to impress the readers.

"The chariot stopped where I stood, thy glance fell on me and thou calmest down with a smile. I felt that the lack of my life had come at last. Then of a sudden thou didn't hold out thy right hand and say what hast thou to give to me?"

Besides being a mystic, Tagore is a man of teachings. He is not a preacher but his poems teaches good lessons to human beings, act as an educator of mankind. This parable, in which the practice of charity is applauded depicts one of the sayings of the Bhagavad Gita, where it is mentioned that the Lord of creation having, in ancient times, emanated mankind together with sacrifice said:

"By this shall ye propagate, be this to you the giver of desires."

Means one gets in proportion to what one sacrifices. One must not always expect favours from others or God but should do whatever he can do for the needy and the unfortunate. The poet here conceived himself as a mendicant and God as a magnificent prince who would be expected to give generous alms to everybody. But the beggar's hopes are belied. The prince comes out of the chariot and suddenly opens his palm before the beggar and asks the beggar as to what he has got to give the prince instead of giving anything himself to the poor beggar. The beggar gives him one of the smallest grains of corn, only to find at the end of the day that the alms collected by him contain one grain of gold. Thus God has rewarded charity.

There is a mystical background also to the episode described here, Kuchela (Sudama) the boyhood friend of Krishna, was living a life of utter poverty. One day he remembered his friend Krishna the Lord of Prosperity and visited him in rags. He offered Krishna some stale corn meal he carried with him. Krishna ate it exhibiting great pleasure and each morsel he took Kuchela grew richer and more richer. On reaching home he found his home flooded with wealth and splendour. This is the might of charity or giving

****

CHAPTER SEVEN

In The Bazaars of Hyderabad

In The Bazaars of Hyderabad
Sarojini Naidu
What do you sell O ye merchants ?
Richly your wares are displayed.
Turbans of crimson and silver,
Tunics of purple brocade,
Mirrors with panels of amber,
Daggers with handles of jade.
What do you weigh, O ye vendors?
Saffron and lentil and rice.
What do you grind, O ye maidens?
Sandalwood, henna, and spice.
What do you call , O ye pedlars?
Chessmen and ivory dice.
What do you make,O ye goldsmiths?
Wristlet and anklet and ring,
Bells for the feet of blue pigeons
Frail as a dragon-fly's wing,
Girdles of gold for dancers,
Scabbards of gold for the king.
What do you cry,O ye fruitmen?

Citron, pomegranate, and plum.
What do you play ,O musicians?
Cithar, sarangi and drum.
what do you chant, O magicians?
Spells for aeons to come.
What do you weave, O ye flower-girls
With tassels of azure and red?
Crowns for the brow of a bridegroom,
Chaplets to garland his bed.
Sheets of white blossoms new-garnered
To perfume the sleep of the dead.

Sarojini Naidu: Biography, Literary Journey, Political Activism & Legacies
Sarojini Naidu

Sarojini Naidu

Sarojini Naidu, famously known as the Nightingale of India or Bharat Kokila, is a monumental figure in Indian history. With equal prowess in the worlds of activism and art, Naidu was a fierce freedom fighter and a celebrated poet of early 20th-century India. In recognition of Naidu's instrumental role in advocating for women's rights, her birth anniversary on the 13 February every year is celebrated as National Women's Day in India.

As India celebrates the 145th birth anniversary of Sarojini Naidu on 13th February 2024, this article of NEXT IAS presents a detailed biography of Sarojini Naidu, including her literary journey, political activism, notable contributions and legacies.

Early Life and Education of Sarojini Naidu

Sarojini Naidu was born on February 13, 1879, in Hyderabad, into a distinguished Bengali Hindu family. Naidu inherited progressive thoughts from her father, Aghorenath Chattopadhyay, who was a progressive thinker and a proponent of education. Her mother Barada Sundari Devi Chattopadhyay was a Bengali poetess, who instilled in her an exceptional aptitude for languages and poetry. It was this blend of scholarly pursuit and poetic talent that sowed the seed for her future endeavors as a nationalist and a poet.

The progressive environment of her family encouraged her education since her childhood. Sarojini Naidu passed the matriculation examination from the University of Madras, achieving the first rank, which was an extraordinary accomplishment at the time, especially for a young girl.

Having completed her early education in India, she set on a path to further her studies abroad, a rare opportunity for Indian women at the time. Her journey of studies abroad included education at King's College (London), followed by that at Girton College (Cambridge).

Her education in England further enriched her understanding of literature and honed her skills as a writer. Moreover, it was during this period that Sarojini Naidu was exposed to the ideas of liberty, democracy, and nationalism. Her interactions with the British and Indian intellectuals in England awakened her political consciousness and she became more acutely aware of the political situation in India and the growing freedom movement. It was this diverse experience in England that laid the groundwork for her future involvement in the literary world as well as India's struggle for independence.

Literary Journey of Sarojini Naidu

Sarojini Naidu's evolution as a poet was a journey marked by early talent, literary exploration, and a deepening engagement with the socio-political issues of her time. She displayed an exceptional talent for writing from a very young age. By the age of 13, she had produced a significant body of literary work, which was compiled as her first collection of poems.

Growing up in a multilingual family, Naidu's early poetry was infused with the rich cultural and linguistic heritage of India. Her education in England gave her exposure to Western literary traditions and the works of prominent poets. This expanded her literary horizons and influenced her thematic and stylistic choices. The result was that her literary works emerged as a perfect fusion of Indian themes with English verse.

Sarojini Naidu's Notable Literary Works

Sarojini Naidu's literary legacy is marked by a collection of works that beautifully capture the essence of Indian culture, landscapes, and the spirit of its freedom struggle.

Her initial works showcased an emotional depth, along with a vivid portrayal of Indian landscapes and life. Her involvement in the national movement influenced her writing, and her poetry began to reflect a stronger sense of nationalism and a subtle critique of colonial rule. Over time, her poetry also began to address social and political issues more directly, particularly those concerning women's rights and women empowerment.

The major literary works of Sarojini Naidu include the following:

- The Golden Threshold: This was Sarojini Naidu's first collection of poems. This was published in 1905 and is named after her family home in Hyderabad.
- The Bird of Time: Published in 1912, this collection features patriotic pieces that reflect Naidu's deep love for her country.
- The Broken Wing: This collection is known for including one of the most famous poems of Naidu "In the Bazaars of Hyderabad".
- The Sceptred Flute: Songs of India: This anthology of Naidu's poems was published after her death and includes verses that artfully weave the essence of Indian tradition with the English language.
- The Feather of The Dawn: Published in 1961, this was edited by her daughter Padmaja Naidu. This collection comprises previously unpublished poems by Sarojini Naidu.

Apart from the above-listed one, her literary works include many other notable poems. Celebrated for their lyrical beauty and patriotic fervor her poems remain a testament to her enduring legacy as "The Nightingale of

India."

Political Activism of Sarojini Naidu

During her time, the nationalistic fervor and growing demand for freedom from British rule were sweeping across India. All these deeply influenced Naidu and she ventured into the Indian freedom movement. Along with making her poetry a powerful medium of propagating nationalism, she took active participation in several movements organized during her time.

Some of the notable involvement and contributions of Sarojini Naidu in the Freedom Struggle are listed below:

- Influence of Gopal Krishna Gokhale: Gopal Krishna Gokhale played a crucial role in drawing Sarojini Naidu closer to the freedom movement. Inspired by his ideals and dedication, Naidu decided to dedicate her life to the cause of India's independence.
- Anti-Partition Movement: She formally joined the Indian national movement during the anti-partition of Bengal in 1905.
- Meeting with Mahatma Gandhi: Her encounter with Mahatma Gandhi further enhanced her engagement in India's Freedom Struggle. Gandhi's philosophy of non-violence and civil disobedience deeply resonated with her, and she became one of his closest associates and supporters.
- Participation in Non-Cooperation Movement: Naidu took an active part in the Non-Cooperation Movement launched in 1920.

  - She was arrested several times during the Non-Cooperation Movement.

- Role in the Indian National Congress: In recognition of her role in the Indian independence movement, Naidu was appointed as the President of the Indian National Congress in Kanpur Session 1925.

  - She was the first Indian woman and overall the second woman (after Annie Besant) to serve as the President of the Indian National Congress.
  - Her presidency marked a significant milestone in recognizing the role of women in the Indian independence movement.

- Participation in Civil Disobedience and Salt Satyagraha: Naidu played a pivotal role in the Civil Disobedience Movement and the Salt Satyagraha of 1930. She led the Dharasana Satyagraha after Gandhi's arrest, showcasing her courage to face colonial repression.
- Second Round Table Conference: Naidu accompanied Gandhi to London for the second Round Table Conference held in 1931.
- Participation in Quit India Movement: Sarojini Naidu registered her participation in Quit India Movement launched in 1942 as well.
- Advocacy for Women's Rights: Naidu is known for championing the cause of women's rights in India. She saw the national movement as an opportunity for women to showcase their strength and hence advocated for women's active participation in the freedom struggle.
- Advocacy Abroad: Naidu traveled to different countries to mobilize international support for India's freedom struggle.

- She also represented India at various international forums, where she advocated for the Indian independence movement and women's rights.

Sarojini Naidu's Advocacy for Women's Rights

Sarojini Naidu's advocacy for women's rights was an essential part of her larger vision for India. Her commitment to the cause of women's emancipation was rooted in her belief in equality and justice, reflecting her broader vision for an independent and progressive India. Naidu's multifaceted efforts in advocating for women's rights can be seen under the following heads:

Inspirational Figure

By achieving a high level of education and actively engaging in political and social causes, Naidu herself emerged as an inspirational figure for Indian women. Her success in the public sphere became a beacon of hope for women across India and inspired them to fight for their emancipation.

Promotion of Women's Education

Understanding the pivotal role of education in empowering women, Naidu advocated for greater access to education for girls. She believed that educated women were crucial not only to India's struggle for independence but also to the nation's progress.

Promotion of Women's Participation

As a prominent leader in the Indian National Congress, Naidu used her position to encourage women's participation in the freedom struggle. Her appointment as the president of the Congress in 1925 itself broke the prevailing gender biases and inspired many women to join the movement.

Women's Indian Association

Naidu assisted Annie Besant in establishing the Women's India Association in 1917. Here, she advocated for women's suffrage and better conditions for women in India.

Legislative Advocacy

Naidu pushed for legislative reforms to improve the status of women in India. She supported laws that aimed at abolishing child marriage and enhancing women's rights in marriage, including property rights.

Public Speaking and Writing

Through her speeches and writings, Naidu addressed the issues faced by women, including the need for political rights, and social equality. She used her eloquence and persuasive power to emphasize the importance of women's roles in shaping modern India.

International Women's Conferences

Sarojini Naidu represented India at international women's conferences, raising awareness about the condition of Indian women and garnering support for their cause. Her international engagement helped link the struggle for women's rights in India with global feminist movements. Thus, in a sense, she highlighted the universal quest for gender equality.

Sarojini Naidu's Roles in Post-Independence India

The period from India's independence in August 1947 until the death of Sarojini Naidu on March 2, 1949, was very short. However, Naidu played some crucial roles even during this brief period.

Governor of the United Provinces

One of Sarojini Naidu's most notable contributions to post-independence India was her appointment as the Governor of the United Provinces (now Uttar Pradesh), a position she held until her death.

- It is to be noted that Naidu is Governor of any state to be appointed as the Governor of any state. This historic appointment not only broke gender barriers but also set a precedent for women's participation in high-level administrative roles in independent India.

Advocacy for Communal Harmony

The events that unfolded after the partition of India in 1947 led to widespread communal violence and displacement. In her capacity as a leader and public figure, Naidu used her eloquence to promote peace and reconciliation among communities.

Promotion of Women's Rights

Even after independence, Naidu continued to promote the cause of women's rights and empowerment. She emphasized that the progress of the newly independent India depended on the progress of its women.

Symbol of National Pride

Naidu remained a symbol of national pride and cultural heritage in post-independence India. Through her writings and public life, Naidu continued to inspire a sense of unity and purpose among Indians during the critical years of nation-building.

Legacies of Sarojini Naidu

Through her myriad contributions, Sarojini Naidu has left a lasting impact on the nation's cultural and political landscape. In contemporary India, her legacy is commemorated through various memorials, institutions, and events. Some of the prominent symbols of her legacy in present India can be seen as follows:

National Women's Day

Recognising the crucial role played by Naidu in advocating for women's rights in India, the Government of

India has declared her birth anniversary on 13 February every year as National Women's Day. It serves as a reminder of the role women have played in shaping India's history and as an inspiration for ongoing efforts toward gender equality and women's empowerment.

Educational Institutions

Several educational institutions have been named after Sarojini Naidu to honor her contributions to education and literature. These include the Sarojini Naidu College for Women in Kolkata, Sarojini Naidu Medical College in Agra, and Sarojini Naidu Government Girls Post Graduate (Autonomous) College, Bhopal.

Literary Commemorations

Naidu's work as a poet is celebrated in literary circles. Literary festivals, poetry readings, and academic conferences often feature sessions dedicated to her work.

Public Memorials and Statues

Public memorials and statues of Sarojini Naidu have been erected in various parts of India, serving as physical reminders of her contributions to the nation.

Government Awards and Recognitions

In recognition of Naidu's role in women empowerment, the Government of India has instituted several awards in her name. These awards recognise women who have made significant contributions in various fields such as arts, culture, and social service.

Cultural Legacy

Sarojini Naidu's life and work have been the subject of various cultural productions, including films, plays, and books. For example, the Film Division of the Ministry of Information and Broadcasting has produced some films based on the biography of Sarojini Naidu.

Significance in Contemporary India

with an ongoing struggle for gender equality and women empowerment, Sarojini Naidu's life and work continue to hold significance in the present time.

Sarojini Naidu's contributions to India's struggle for independence and her role in the early years of post-independence India remain immortalized in Indian history. Naidu's life and work continue to inspire generations of Indians, particularly women, to contribute to the welfare and progress of their country.

In The Bazaars of Hyderabad: Stanza-wise Summary

What do you sell O ye merchants?

Richly your wares are displayed.

Turbans of crimson and silver,

Tunics of Purple brocade,

Mirrors with panels of Amber,

Daggers with handles of jade.

The poem begins with the poet's question to the merchants about what they are selling. She sees that the goods are displayed nicely to attract the buyers. The merchants reply that they are selling crimson (deep red) and silver coloured turbans, purple brocade tunics, mirrors with amber-frame and daggers with handles made of jade (a green stone).

What do you weigh, O ye vendors?

Saffron and lentil and rice.

What do you grind, O ye maidens?

Sandalwood, henna, and spice.

What do you call, O ye pedlars?

Chessmen and ivory dice.

The poet then visits the vendors, the maidens and the pedlars (salesmen). She asks the vendors what they are weighing for sale. The vendors reply that they are weighing saffron, lentil and rice. The poet then asks the maiden girls what they are grinding. the reply comes that they are grinding sandalwood, henna and spices. And now the pedlars are asked what they are calling as their trade cry. They say that they are selling chessmen and dice made from ivory for the game of chess.

What do you make, O ye goldsmiths?
Wristlet and anklet and ring,
Bells for the feet of blue pigeons,
Frail as a dragon-fly's wing,
Girdles of gold for dancers,
Scabbards of gold for the king.

The poet now goes up to the goldsmiths and asks them what they are making. They are making wristlet, anklet and ring to adorn us and bells to be tied to the feet of blue pigeons. And the bells are as thin and lightweight as the wings of a dragonfly. They are also making golden girdles for the dancers and golden sheaths for keeping the king's swords.

What do you cry, O ye, fruitmen?
Citron, pomegranate, and plum.
What do you play, O musicians?
Sitar, sarangi and drum.
What do you chant, O magicians?
Spells for aeons to come.

The poet in the poem In The Bazaars of Hyderabad now asks the fruit sellers what fruits are they selling. They answer that there are citron, pomegranate and plum. Now as the poet asks the musicians what instruments they are play, they reply that they are playing on sitar, sarangi and drum. After that poet goes to the magicians and asks them what they are chanting. The reply comes,he is chanting the spells to bring in aeons (a divine power) who would help him perform his magical tricks.

What do you weave, O ye flower-girls?
With tassels of azure and red?
Crowns for the brow of a bridegroom,
Chaplets to garland his bed.
Sheets of white blossoms, new-garnered
To perfume the sleep of the dead.

In the last stanza of the poem the poet asks the flower girls what they are weaving with the azure (deep blue) and red tassels (strands of flower). The flower girls are making garlands for the bride and the groom and to adorn their bed for the wedding night. They are also making sheets of newly brought white flowers for use on the dead man's grave for fragrance.

Thus the poet Sarojini Naidu represents an Indian market to give us a sense of the rich Indian heritage. This poem was her protest against the European products and an appreciation of our own goods.

Explain the role of vendors, pedlars and maidens in the poem

The vendors, pedlars and maidens play an important role in the poem to present an outstanding picture of an Indian market. The poet's motive was to show the diversity and self-sufficiency of an Indian market in British India. The native Indian culture and tradition are glorified and showcased in the poem. And these people like pedlars and vendors are an inseparable part of that picture. Not only the vendors, pedlars and maidens, but also the magician, the musicians, the goldsmiths, the flower girls – all play the same role in the poem 'In the Bazaars of Hyderabad'.

Why does the poet use the word 'cry' to refer to the fruitmen's call in the poem 'In The Bazaars of Hyderabad'?

The fruitmen generally shout their trade cry very loudly to attract more buyers. So this is only appropriate to use the word 'cry' to refer to their call. It was very much necessary to use the right words to represent the real picture of the market well before our eyes.

Who sells expensive board games in the poem 'In the Bazaars of Hyderabad' by Sarojini Naidu? What indicates they are expensive?

The pedlars are selling those expensive board games, the chessmen and the ivory dice.

The dices are made of ivory. That certainly makes them expensive.

The expensive board games suggest that some wealthy people like kings and nawabs had a lot of leisure hours and they enjoyed spending those hours by playing chess. Moreover, it represents their luxurious lifestyle, immense wealth of the city and the rich cultural tradition of the place.

Where do you think is Sarojini Naidu's poem "In the Bazaars of Hyderabad" set?

Or, What is the setting of the poem "In the Bazaars of Hyderabad"?

Naidu's poem "In the Bazaars of Hyderabad" is set in a traditional Indian market in Hyderabad in British India, i.e., before independence. It is unlike a modern supermarket. The sellers used to bring mostly their home-made products and sell them in the bazaar shouting their trade-cry.

What are the colours mentioned in the poem 'In the bazaars of Hyderabad'? What effect do the colours create?

The colors mentioned in the poem are crimson and silver of turbans, purple of tunic brocade, green of jade, saffron, yellow of lentils, the golden colour of jewellery, azure and red of tassels and white of blossoms.

These variety of colours create cheerful and positive vibes in our minds and they represent the vibrancy of an Indian market. This vibrancy is what the poet wanted to show.

In Sarojini Naidu's poem "In the Bazaars of Hyderabad", the objects sold by the goldsmiths indicate the immense wealth of the city. Discuss.

Or, What kind of bells are tied to the pigeon's feet? What does this tell you about the Indian society?

Naidu's poem shows that the rich people of Hyderabad not only bought gold ornaments like wristlet, anklet and ring to adorn themselves, but also fancy things like delicate bells for the feet of blue pigeons, girdles for the dancers and scabbards of gold for the king. This indicates the immense wealth of the city where people did not hesitate to buy luxury items made of gold. It also indicates to the rich cultural tradition of the society.

How do the flowers connect life and death as indicated in Sarojini Naidu's poem 'In The Bazaars of Hyderabad'? / What role does the flowers play at a wedding and a death ceremony?

The flowers are used to adorn the bride and the groom and to decorate their bed for the wedding night. This glorifies life. But the same flowers are used to perfume the deathbed of a man. Thus the flowers connect life and death, as the poet has presented it in the poem.

What are the magicians doing in the bazaar as depicted in the poem "In the Bazaars of Hyderabad" by Sarojini Naidu?

The magicians are trying to sell their tricks and performances to the people present there.

They woo their customers by chanting the "spells for aeons to come".

What do the goldsmiths make and for whom?

Goldsmiths make-

1. Gold ornaments like anklet, wristlet and rings.

2. Golden delicate and light-weight bells for pigeon's feet

3. Gold waist chains called girdles for dancers

4. gold sword covers known as sheaths for kings

How is Sarojini Naidu's poem 'In The Bazaars of Hyderabad' Indian in content and presentation?

Sarojini Naidu's poem 'In the Bazaars of Hyderabad' is, no doubt, an Indian poem in its thought and spirit. The variety of professions and the products are all Indian. The Products like purple brocade tunics, amber mirror-panels and jade dagger-handles represents the rich cultural tradition of India. The magician chanting spells, musicians playing sitar and sarangi, pedlars selling chessmen and ivory dice, maidens selling sandalwood and henna – all are essentially Indian.

The poet has presented a typical Indian bazaar where people from different kinds of profession have gathered to sell their products or show their skills to earn a living. Again, the use of the words like 'bazaar', 'sitar' and 'sarangi' , the use of simile like 'frail as a dragon-fly's wing' are Indian in their origin and characteristic. Last but not the least, the very mention of the city of Hyderabad declares it as a poem essentially Indian.

What quality of the king does the word 'scabbard' suggest in Sarojini Naidu's poem 'In the Bazaars of Hyderabad'?

From the word 'scabbard' we understand that the king was very rich and kept his sword in a gold scabbard and protected his kingdom.

In Sarojini Naidu's poem 'In the Bazaars of Hyderabad' how do the magicians announce themselves? What do they claim for the thing they sell?

As told in Naidu's poem In the Bazaars of Hyderabad, the magicians announce themselves with their chanting of spells to bring in the aeons.

For the things they sell — the magical arts they perform — the magicians claim out rapt attention and our awe.

Comment on the use of rural touch in Sarojini Naidu's poem 'In the Bazaars of Hyderabad'.

Sarojini Naidu's poem 'In the Bazaars of Hyderabad' essentially represents the rural India in the twentieth century. The poem depicts a rural market with all its buzz and vibrancy where people from different professions have gathered to sell their products or to showcase their skills.

Here we see the vendors selling food grains, goldsmiths selling their delicate ornaments, merchants selling valuable objects, maidens grinding sandalwood, henna and spice, fruitmen shouting their trade cry, musicians playing sitar, sarangi and drum, magicians chanting spells and flower girls weaving tassels and chaplets of flowers. People from all these various professions gathering at a bazaar to earn their living or just to pursue their family tradition is definitely a scene of a rural market that is very different from a modern-day supermarket in an urban area. Moreover, all the products available here are native products made from natural objects. Nothing is artificial, machine-made or imported here as we see them in an urban market. This too contributes to the rural touch of the poem.

Why do you think the poem In the Bazaars of Hyderabad by Sarojini Naidu ends with a mention of people who have died?

Mentioning the sheets of white flowers 'to perfume the sleep of the dead' might have an implication that the bazaars of Hyderabad had everything that a man needed, not only in his lifetime, but also after his death. After all, the poet's message was to emphasise the diversity and self-sufficiency of an Indian market in British India.

What are the professions named in Sarojini Naidu's poem 'In the Bazaars of Hyderabad'?

The poet has mentioned various professions to create a complete picture of a Bazaar or market in British India. There are the merchants, vendors, maidens grinding sandalwood and henna, pedlars, goldsmiths, fruitmen, musicians, magicians and the flower-girls.

****

CHAPTER EIGHT

LITERARY TERMS

LITERARY TERMS

SONNET:

A sonnet is a type of poem consisting fourteen-line. Traditionally, the fourteen lines of a sonnet consist of an octave (or two quatrains making up a stanza of 8 lines) and a sestet (a stanza of six lines). Sonnets generally use a meter of iambic pentameter, and follow a set rhyme scheme. Within these general guidelines for what makes a sonnet, there are a wide variety of variations. The two most common sonnet variations are the Italian sonnet (also called a Petrarchan sonnet), and the English sonnet (also called a Shakespearean sonnet). The main difference between the Italian and English sonnet is in the rhyme schemes they use.

The Petrarchan sonnet characteristically treats its theme in two parts. The first eight lines, the octave, state a problem, ask a question, or express an emotional tension. The last six lines, the sestet, resolve the problem, answer the question, or relieve the tension. The octave is rhymed *abbaabba*. The rhyme scheme of the sestet varies; it may be *cdecde, cdccdc,* or *cdedce.* The Petrarchan sonnet became a major influence on European poetry. It soon became naturalized in Spain, Portugal, and France and was introduced to Poland, whence it spread to other Slavic literatures. In most cases the form was adapted to the staple metre of the language—e.g., the alexandrine (12-syllable iambic line) in France and iambic pentameter in English.

The sonnet was introduced to England, along with other Italian verse forms, by Sir Thomas Wyatt and Henry Howard, earl of Surrey, in the 16th century. The new forms precipitated the great Elizabethan flowering of lyric poetry, and the period marks the peak of the sonnet's English popularity. In the course of adapting the Italian form to a language less rich in rhymes, the Elizabethans gradually arrived at the distinctive English sonnet, which is composed of three quatrains, each having an independent rhyme scheme, and is ended with a rhymed couplet.

The rhyme scheme of the English sonnet is abab cdcd efef gg. Its greater number of rhymes makes it a less demanding form than the Petrarchan sonnet, but this is offset by the difficulty presented by the couplet, which must summarize the impact of the preceding quatrains with the compressed force of a Greek epigram.

The typical Elizabethan use of the sonnet was in a sequence of love poems in the manner of Petrarch. Although each sonnet was an independent poem, partly conventional in content and partly self-revelatory, the sequence had the added interest of providing something of a narrative development. Among the notable Elizabethan sequences are Sir Philip Sidney's Astrophel and Stella (1591), Samuel Daniel's Delia (1592), Michael Drayton's Idea's Mirrour (1594), and Edmund Spenser's Amoretti (1591). The last-named work uses a common variant of the sonnet (known as Spenserian) that follows the English quatrain and couplet pattern but resembles the Italian in using a linked rhyme scheme: abab bcbc cdcd ee. Perhaps the greatest of all sonnet sequences is Shakespeare's, addressed to a young man and a "dark lady." In these sonnets the supposed love story is of less interest than the underlying reflections on time and art, growth and decay, and fame and fortune.

In its subsequent development the sonnet was to depart even further from themes of love. By the time John Donne wrote his religious sonnets (c. 1610) and Milton wrote sonnets on political and religious subjects or on personal themes such as his blindness (i.e., "When I consider how my light is spent"), the sonnet had been extended to embrace nearly all the subjects of poetry.

It is the virtue of this short form that it can range from "light conceits of lovers" to considerations of life, time, death, and eternity, without doing injustice to any of them. Even during the Romantic era, in spite of the emphasis on freedom and spontaneity, the sonnet forms continued to challenge major poets. Many English writers—including William Wordsworth, John Keats, and Elizabeth Barrett Browning—continued to write Petrarchan sonnets. With few exceptions, Italian sonnets and early English sonnets are about unrequited love. Then, in the 17th century, John Donne began writing religious sonnets, and shortly thereafter John Milton began using the form for everything from satirical poems to more serious poems of soul-searching and reflection. In the 19th century, the sonnet's popularity among poets around the globe soared, such that by the end of the century so many variations had been made to the form that it was seen as well-suited to any subject matter. Today, as a result, sonnets don't have to take any particular subject as their focus.

LYRIC:

The word lyric comes from the lyre, an ancient Greek portable harp frequently used by performers. Lyrical poetry was originally meant to be set to music and performed. With the advent of the printing press, performed poetry took a backseat to written works, but since the mid-20th century and the ubiquitous access to popular music, people are as likely to hear a lyric as they are to read it.

In ancient Greece, poets performed their work with musical accompaniment, usually in the form of lyres, other stringed instruments, or panpipes. Some of the earliest lyrics poems were compiled by the library of Alexandria, including the work of Sappho. These traditions were also carried on by a few poets in ancient Rome.

In short a Lyric is a type of poetry that expresses the poet's feelings, emotions, and personal thoughts, characterized by subjectivity, immediacy, musicality, and briefness. It can also be the words or text of a song, especially those that express the singer's emotions or thoughts. In general, the core idea of "lyric" is to convey emotion, thought, or feeling through language, whether in poetry or music.

As early as the 7th century, the first incarnations of the ghazal, a type of lyric poem composed of couplets, began to appear in Arabia. Around the 11th century, troubadours started making their way through Europe. As with the ghazal, the troubadours' lyric works often concerned courtly love. In 12th-century Italy, the poet Petrarch developed the sonnet, a 14-line poem that Edmund Spencer and William Shakespeare would modify and popularize in the 15th century.

The popularity of lyric poetry saw peaks and lulls from that point up to the beginning of the 20th century, when modernists like T.S. Elliot and William Carlos Williams began to criticize the genre. In the 1950s and '60s, confessional poets like Sylvia Plath and Anne Sexton brought lyric poetry back into fashion and made it almost a form of activism by discussing sex, mental illness, and other taboo topics.

Here are some common types of lyric poetry:

1. Ode: A formal, expressive poem that praises a person, place, or thing.

2. Ballad: A narrative poem that tells a story in verse, often with a folkloric or legendary theme.

3. Sonnet: A 14-line poem with a specific rhyme scheme, exploring a single idea or emotion.

4. Elegy: A poem that mourns the loss of someone or something.

5. Limerick: A humorous, five-line poem with a specific rhyme scheme.

6. Tanka: A Japanese poem that explores themes of love, nature, or the seasons.

7. Haiku: A Japanese poem that captures a moment in time or a feeling.

8. Free Verse: A poem that doesn't follow a specific rhyme or meter, instead using natural speech rhythms.

9. Ghazal: A Middle Eastern poem that explores themes of love, spirituality, and social issues.

10. Villanelle: A poem with 19 lines, featuring a repeating refrain and specific rhyme scheme.

11. Sapphic: A poem that explores themes of love and desire, often with a specific meter.

12. Pindaric: A poem that celebrates a person or achievement, often with a specific structure.

EPIC:

It is imperative to know the etymology of the word epic. The word epic has been derived from the Greek word epikos, which means a word, song or speech. An epic is well-defined as a long story in verse dwelling upon an important theme in a most elegant style and language. According to Webster's New World Dictionary, "epic is a long narrative poem in a dignified style about the deeds of a traditional or historical hero or heroes; typically a poem like Iliad or the Odyssey with certain formal characteristics." An epic is much like a ballad in all its features.

However, its length is one thing that differentiates the epic from the ballad. An epic is a long narrative in verse, while a ballad is a short story in verse.

Britannica Encyclopedia explains the word epic as:

"epic, long narrative poem recounting heroic deeds. ... literary usage, the term encompasses both oral and written compositions. The prime examples of the oral epic are Homer's Iliad and Odyssey."

There are several characteristics of an epic that distinguish it from other forms of poetry. They are discussed below:

The first and foremost characteristic of an epic is its bulky size. An epic is an extensive and prolonged narrative in verse. Usually, every single epic has been broken down into multiple books. For example, Homer's epics are divided into twenty-four books. Similarly, John Milton's Paradise Lost has been divided into twelve books.

Another essential feature of an epic is the fact that it dwells upon the achievements of a historical or traditional hero or a person of national or international significance. Every epic extolls the valour, deeds, bravery, character and personality of a person who has incredible physical and mental traits.

Exaggeration is also an important part of an epic. The poet uses hyperbole to reveal the prowess of a hero. He doesn't think twice about using exaggeration to make an impression on the audience.

Supernaturalism is a must-have feature of every epic. Without having to use supernatural elements, no epic would certainly produce awe and wonder. There are certainly gods, demons, angels, fairies, and use of supernatural forces like natural catastrophes in every epic. Milton's Paradise Lost, Homer's Iliad, Beowulf and Spenser's Faerie Queen are replete with supernatural elements.

Morality is a key characteristic of an epic. The poet's foremost purpose in writing an epic is to give a moral lesson to his readers. For instance, Johan Milton's Paradise Lost is a perfect example in this regard. The poet wants to justify God's ways to man through Adam's story. This is the most didactic theme of the epic.

The theme of each epic is sublime, elegant, and has universal significance. It may not be an insignificant theme that is only limited to the personality or the locality of the poet. It deals with the entire humanity. Thus, John Milton's Paradise Lost is a great example in this regard. The theme of this epic is certainly of great importance and deals with humanity as a whole. Its theme is to justify the ways of God to man.

Invocation to the Muse is another important quality of an epic. The poet, at the very beginning of the epic, seeks the help of the Muse while writing his epic. Look at the beginning lines of the Iliad, Odyssey and Paradise Lost.

he diction of every epic is lofty, grand and elegant. No trivial, common or colloquial language is used in epics. The poet tries to use sublime words to describe the events.

The use of epic simile is another feature of an epic. Epic simile is a far-fetched comparison between two objects, which runs through many lines to describe the valour, bravery and gigantic stature of the hero. It is also called the Homeric simile.

Some classic examples of epics include:
- Homer's "The Iliad" and "The Odyssey"
- Virgil's "The Aeneid"
- Dante's "The Divine Comedy"
- John Milton's "Paradise Lost"

ELEGY:

An elegy is a poem of serious reflection, especially one mourning the loss of someone who died. Elegies are defined by their subject matter, and don't have to follow any specific form in terms of meter, rhyme, or structure.

The ancient Greeks established a tradition of "elegeia," which refers to a poetic verse of couplets about subjects such as death, loss, love, and battle. This tradition was adopted by Roman conquerors who formulated elegies in Latin and addressed similar topics as Greek elegeia but added erotic and mythological themes as well.

The Renaissance brought a revival of elegy poems and their introduction to English literature. English poets focused their elegiacal verse primarily on death and loss of a loved one.

Classical elegiac poetry was generally structured in couplets. Since the eighteenth century, stanzas within elegy poems typically feature a quatrain, written in iambic pentameter with an ABAB rhyme scheme. However, this structure is only suggestive, as many poets compose elegies with different meter and rhyme scheme. In fact, most contemporary elegies have no set or formal structure at all.

However, elegiacal poetry can address many themes other than loss of life and grief. Here are some common examples of theme in elegy:

- death and its inevitability and/or universality
- personal loss
- humankind and nature
- memory and/or the past
- Nostalgia for youth
- isolation
- devotion
- society
- loss of love
- death of influential leader, writer, or other public figures/heroes.

Examples of elegies include:
- Thomas Gray's "Elegy Written in a Country Churchyard"
- Walt Whitman's "When Lilacs Last in the Dooryard Bloom'd" (for President Lincoln)
- W.H. Auden's "In Memory of W.B. Yeats"
- Mary Elizabeth Frye's "Do Not Stand at My Grave and Weep"

ODE:

An ode is a type of poem that is written in praise of a person, place, object, or idea. The word ode first appeared in English in the 1580s. It comes from the Middle French ode via the Late Latin ode, meaning "lyric song," which was derived from the Ancient Greek aeidein, meaning "to sing or chant."

Odes originated as Greek choral songs performed at religious festivals. They recounted stories concerning heroes, gods, and victories in battle. The original odes were set to music and followed a specific, complex three-part structure utilizing a strophe (the first section), an antistrophe (the second section), and an epode (the final section).

The form was adapted by Latin poets who loosened the structure and wrote in a less formal tone. Eventually, the ode was popularized in Renaissance England. In the English tradition, the term ode was used more loosely and meant either a poem of praise or a poem containing an emotional outburst.

According to former U.S. Poet Laureate Robert Hass, "By the nineteenth century [the ode] was a longish lyric poem, often with an elaborate stanza structure written in lines of varying and irregular length and often with different formal patterns in different parts."

The characteristics of an ode include:

1. Expressive and lyrical language: Odes use vivid, descriptive language to express deep emotions.

2. Formal structure: Odes often follow a specific rhyme or meter, such as the Pindaric or Horatian ode.

3. Elevated tone: Odes have a dignified, elevated tone, often expressing admiration or reverence.

4. Lengthy and elaborate: Odes can be lengthy and elaborate, with multiple stanzas and complex metaphors.

5. Personal and emotional: Odes often express the poet's personal feelings and emotions.

6. Rich imagery and symbolism: Odes frequently employ rich imagery and symbolism to convey meaning.

Types of odes include:

1. Pindaric ode: A formal, expressive ode with a specific structure and rhyme scheme.

2. Horatian ode: A more informal, conversational ode that explores themes and ideas.

3. Keatsian ode: A sensual, beautiful ode that explores themes of beauty and truth.

Examples of odes include:

1. John Keats' "Ode to a Nightingale"

2. Percy Bysshe Shelley's "Ode to the West Wind"

3. Pindar's "Olympian Odes"

4. Horace's "Odes"

Odes can be written in various forms and styles, but always express a deep sense of admiration and praise.

BALLAD:

The word 'ballad' is pronounced 'bal - lad'. 'Ballad' is derived from an old French word, balade, which means a song that people dance to. The etymology of balade can be dated even further back to the Latin word, ballare, which means to dance.

Ballads were traditionally sung or recited within rural communities in a form known as the traditional or folk ballad. Ballads originated as a poetic form in Europe around the 14th century. The classical form was popularised orally by wandering minstrels and began to appear in print by the late 15th century. The content of ballads was often a play on local legends from wandering minstrels of medieval times. The poetic form changed and developed with the introduction of the literary ballad, which is a written form of ballad that embodies the spirit of the traditional ballad.

A ballad is a form of narrative verse that is considered either poetic or musical. As a literary device, a ballad is a narrative poem, typically consisting of a series of four-line stanzas. Ballads were originally sung or recited as an oral tradition among rural societies and were often anonymous retellings of local legends and stories by wandering minstrels in the Middle Ages. These traditional or "folk" ballads are sometimes referred to as "popular" ballads. Literary ballads are deliberate creations by poets in imitation of the form and spirit of a traditional ballad.

In short, a ballad is a narrative poem or song that tells a story, often with a folkloric or legendary theme. The characteristics of a ballad include:

1. Narrative structure: Ballads tell a story, often with a clear beginning, middle, and end.

2. Quatrains and rhyme: Ballads typically consist of four-line stanzas (quatrains) with a consistent rhyme scheme.

3. Simple language: Ballads use simple, direct language to convey the story.

4. Folkloric or legendary theme: Ballads often draw on folklore, legends, or historical events.

5. Emotional focus: Ballads frequently focus on emotions, such as love, loss, or tragedy.

6. Repetition and refrain: Ballads often feature repetition, such as a repeated chorus or refrain.

7. Musical quality: Ballads are often meant to be sung or recited, with a strong emphasis on rhythm and meter.

Types of ballads include:

1. Traditional ballad: Passed down orally, often with unknown authors.

2. Literary ballad: Written by a specific author, often with a more formal structure.

3. Folk ballad: Focuses on everyday life and folkloric themes.

4. Romantic ballad: Emphasizes emotion, beauty, and the supernatural.

Examples of ballads include:

1. "The Ballad of Reading Gaol" by Oscar Wilde

2. "The Rime of the Ancient Mariner" by Samuel Taylor Coleridge

3. "La Belle Dame sans Merci" by John Keats

4. "Scarborough Fair" (traditional)

Ballads have been a popular form of storytelling for centuries, and continue to be enjoyed today in many forms.

DRAMATIC MONOLOGUE:

A dramatic monologue is a form of poetry in which a single speaker speaks to a silent listener or listeners. This speaker reveals his thoughts, feelings, motivations, and experiences in a specific situation or moment. Dramatic monologues are commonly used in poetry and drama. This offers a powerful way to explore a character's inner thoughts and emotions. Some famous examples include Robert Browning's "My Last Duchess" and T.S. Eliot's "The Love Song of J. Alfred Prufrock."

Characteristics of Dramatic Monologue: A Dramatic monologue is a unique form of poetry or literature where a character delivers a speech or narrative to an audience. Some key characteristics include.

Single Speaker: There's typically only one character speaking throughout the entire piece. He reveals his thoughts, feelings, motivations, and experiences in a specific situation or moment.

Silent Listener: The speaker addresses someone, whether an individual, a group, or even the reader. This audience or listener always remains silent.

Revealing Nature: It reveals the speaker's thoughts, emotions, motives, and often their flaws. This provides a deep insight into their mentality.

Abrupt Beginning: A dramatic monologue starts abruptly without any introduction.

Use of Colloquial Language: Colloquial Language means conversational language. In a dramatic monologue, the speaker seems to speak with its listeners.

Exploration of Themes: Dramatic monologues often delve into identity, morality, guilt, love, or societal issues. This uses the character's speech to explore and discuss these topics.

Use of Literary Devices: Poetic devices such as meter, rhyme, and imagery are employed to enhance the emotional impact and rhythm of the monologue.

Character Development: Through the monologue, the character's personality, background, and internal conflicts are revealed. This leads to a deeper understanding of who he is.

****

Rhetorical Devices

The 20 Most Common Rhetorical Devices (With Examples)

The phrase rhetorical devices might ring a bell to some. Maybe you vaguely remember hearing about them in an English class that you took years ago. But you probably haven't thought about them since. That's totally understandable, but whether we know it or not, rhetorical devices play a surprisingly large role in our daily speech. Sometimes we use them without even realizing it. Whether they're used to illustrate sound, order or meaning (we'll explain all these in a bit), rhetorical devices are widely used across the board, especially in advertising and marketing. Without further ado, we'd like to share our list of the 20 most common rhetorical devices that you can use to impress your friends and family or win a free round of drinks at the next trivia night at your local bar.

What Are Rhetorical Devices?

Before we dive into the different types of rhetorical devices, we should probably review what exactly they are. "Rhetorical devices" refer to figures of speech that are used to achieve a certain effect. Essentially, they're a way to deviate from everyday language by taking advantage of the power of words.

Words have connotative value: on one hand, they have their denotation, which is their true and correct meaning. On the other hand, words have a set of meanings that are generally attributed to them. For example, the word "heart" literally refers to the organ at the center of your circulatory system. But it can also have a wide variety of connotations or alternative meanings: a person "with a good heart" is someone who's kind and helpful to others. The "heart" of a system is its center, and someone who is "lionhearted" is extremely brave. Rhetorical devices don't use just one meaning or connotation; they also take advantage of different word orders and structures.

Rhetorical devices are most commonly used in literature, but they can also appear in the most unexpected places. They're an intrinsic part of language, and they've probably been around since the beginning of language itself. Even in Ancient Rome, rhetoric students studied the art of classifying words. Early examples of rhetorical devices can even be found in the Bible.

Rhetorical devices can be roughly classified into three different groups:

- Sound-related rhetorical devices: these figures of speech take advantage of a word or phrase's rhythmic or phonetic sound. The most famous examples are alliteration, assonance and puns.
- Order-related rhetorical devices: these devices modify the normal order of words within a phrase or sentence. The most well-known examples are anaphoras, anastrophes, asyndeton, chiasmus, omissions, hyperbaton and polysyndeton.
- Meaning-related rhetorical devices: these types of devices use the word's semantic aspect, or their

meaning. Some examples are hyperbole, litotes, metaphors, metonymy, oxymorons, similes, synecdoche and synesthesia.

What Is Figurative Language?

To understand the many rhetorical devices that exist in the English language, it's important that we first discuss figurative language. Figurative language is the form of communication that rhetorical devices fall under. More specifically, it is when words and phrases stray from their strict, dictionary definition to create new meanings. Most commonly, figurative language is used in poetry and other creative prose. However, it also is used in everyday language in the form of expressions or to refer to something without directly saying it.

Take the expression "the news hit me like a ton of bricks". Figuratively speaking, it's used to quantify the impact of a piece of news on someone. However, when taken literally, this expression doesn't make much sense. To note the obvious, the news itself doesn't carry physical weight and it's also not actually hitting anyone, as it's a concept. Additionally, there is of course no ton of bricks hitting the person in question,which is where the importance of the preposition "like" comes in. The use of "like" in this sentence ultimately changes the meaning and makes this sentence identifiable as a "simile". A simile is one of the many forms that figurative language takes. These forms are better known as rhetorical devices, so let's get into it.

Sound-Related Rhetorical Devices

Alliteration

Alliteration refers to repeating a sound or a series of similar consonant sounds at the beginning of two or more words.

Examples of alliteration:

- How much wood could a woodchuck chuck if a woodchuck could chuck wood?
- Trick or treat!
- "From forth the fatal loins of these two foes . . ." — William Shakespeare

Assonance

Assonance resembles rhyming. It positions two similar sounding words together that have the same vowels (but not the same consonants).

Examples of assonance:

- "And so all the night-tide, I lie down by the side of my darling-my darling-my life and my bride" — Edgar Allen Poe
- "The rain in Spain stays mainly on the plain." — *My Fair Lady*

Onomatopoeia

Onomatopoeia is one of the most famous rhetorical devices. It refers to reproducing the sound of an object (like a machine) or an animal.

Examples of onomatopoeia:

- *Chitty Chitty Bang Bang* (a book written by Ian Fleming, the title of which refers to the sound a car makes)
- "Meow meow." — a cat

Puns

Puns are a common play on words that use words with similar sounds but radically different meanings.

Examples of puns:

- "Denial ain't just a river in Egypt." — Mark Twain
- "We had breakfast in the town of Soda, pop. 1001." — Vladimir Nabokov

Order-Related Rhetorical Devices

Anaphora

An anaphora is the repetition of one or more words within one or more consecutive verses or sentences.

Examples of anaphora:

- "It was the best of times, it was the worst of times..." — Mark Twain
- "So let freedom ring from the prodigious hilltops of New Hampshire. Let freedom ring from the mighty mountains of New York. Let freedom ring from the heightening Alleghenies of Pennsylvania..." — Martin Luther King
- "Ask not what your country can do for you — ask what you can do for your country." — John F. Kennedy

Anastrophe

Derived from Greek, the term anastrophe means "inversion" and is achieved by inverting the usual order of two words.

Examples of anastrophe:

- "The greatest teacher, failure is." — Yoda
- "Certain seeds it will not nurture, certain fruit it will not bear..." — Toni Morrison

- "To thine own self be true." — William Shakespeare

Antithesis

Many rhetorical devices have fancy names that can be difficult to remember. There's a reason why technical jargon is usually used only by literature students and aficionados. Some terms are used so often that they've become commonplace in everyday speech, however. Antithesis is one of these words. Simply put, antithesis refers to juxtaposing two words with opposite meanings. In layman's terms, it refers to some sort of contrast (like contrasting ideas.)

Examples of antithesis:

- "Any customer can have a car painted any color that he wants, as long as it is black." — Henry Ford
- "To err is human; to forgive divine." -Alexander Pope

Asyndeton

Asyndeton is a list of words that are connected by using punctuation instead of conjunctions like "and" or "or."

Examples of asyndeton:

- "That government of the people, by the people, for the people, shall not perish from the earth." — Abraham Lincoln
- "I came, I saw, I conquered." — Julius Caesar

Chiasmus

Chiasmus is the crossed arrangement of two words or groups of words according to the AB-BA format.

Examples of chiasmus:

- "The art of progress is to preserve order amid change and to preserve change amid order." — Alfred North Whitehead
- "And these tend inward to me, and I tend outward to them." — Walt Whitman
- When the going gets tough, the tough get going.

Omission

Omission is the elimination of one or more words that remain understood despite being removed.

Examples of omission:

- "Hope is a thing with feathers/That perches in the soul." — Emily Dickinson
- "And he to England shall along with you." — William Shakespeare

Hyperbaton

Not to be confused with anastrophe, hyperbaton consists of distancing a word from the word that it should be placed closer to.

Examples of hyperbaton:

- "Object there was none. Passion there was none. I loved the old man." -Edgar Allen Poe
- "One swallow does not a summer make, nor one fine day." — Aristotle

Polysyndenton

Polysyndeton is the exact opposite of asyndeton. It's a series of words linked by conjunction words.

Examples of polysyndeton:

- "Lions and tigers and bears, oh my!" — *The Wizard of Oz*
- "I said, 'Who killed him?' and he said, 'I don't know who killed him but he's dead all right,' and it was dark and there was water standing in the street and no lights and windows broke and boats all up in the town and trees blown down and everything all blown and I got a skiff and went out and found my boat where I had her inside Mango Key and she was all right only she was full of water." — Ernest Hemingway

Meaning-Related Rhetorical Devices

Hyperbole

Hyperbole is achieved by exaggerating a reality through expressions that amplify it to an extreme.

Examples of hyperbole:

- "A day was twenty-four hours long but seemed longer. There was no hurry, for there was nowhere to go, nothing to buy and no money to buy it with, nothing to see outside the boundaries of Maycomb County." — *To Kill a Mockingbird*
- "It's a slow burg. I spent a couple of weeks there one day." — Carl Sandburg
- "At that time Bogota was a remote, lugubrious city where an insomniac rain had been falling since the beginning of the 16th century." — Gabriel García Márquez

Litotes

Litotes is the affirmation of something by negating the opposite. It's used, for example, to mitigate the harshness of an expression or a situation.

Examples of litotes:

- It's not rocket science.
- He isn't the brightest bulb in the bunch.

Metaphors

Metaphors are one of the most famous rhetorical devices. Metaphors use words or phrases to indicate something that isn't often denoted by that word or phrase. Metaphors can sometimes be confused with similes, metonymy or synecdoche, but each of these devices have their own unique characteristics.

Examples of metaphors:

- Daniel is a sheep. (Meaning, Daniel follows other people easily.)
- "All the world's a stage, and all the men and women merely players." — William Shakespeare

Metonymy

Metonymy is the exchange of two words that have close reasoning or are closely related in terms of their subject.

Examples of metonymy:

- "I'm reading Sartre." (I'm not reading the word Sartre; I'm reading a piece written by philosopher Jean-Paul Sartre)
- "England beat Italy 2-0." (the soccer team representing England beat the team representing Italy)
- "Let's go get a pint." (a pint in this case refers to some sort of alcoholic drink)

Oxymorons

An oxymoron juxtaposes two words with opposite meanings.

Examples of oxymorons:

- Parting is such sweet sorrow."
- *Big Little Lies* (the title of a book by Liane Moriarty)
- "I am a deeply superficial person." — Andy Warhol

Similes

Similes are very similar to metaphors. In this case, the comparison is made through adverbs or adverbial phrases, most notably "like" or "as."
Examples of similes:

- You're working like a dog.
- He's dead as a doornail.
- The news hit me like a ton of bricks.

Synecdoche

Synecdoche is always mentioned in conjunction with metonymy. These two rhetorical devices are very similar. However, while metonymy substitutes one word or phrase with another that has a close logical or material proximity, synecdoche substitutes a word or phrase with another term representing a part of it (or vice versa: it uses a broader term to refer to something that it's a part of). Metonymy expresses a qualitative relationship between the two terms, while synecdoche represents a quantitative relationship.
Examples of synecdoche:

- The feline attacked the antelope. (in this case, the broader term feline, the family that the animal belongs to, is used to denote a tiger)
- "Friends, Romans, countrymen, lend me your ears" — William Shakespeare

- Brain drain (when people educated in their native country seek opportunities in other countries. In this case, it's not the brains physically leaving the country but the academic talent)

Synesthesia

Synesthesia is a type of metaphor that's created by connecting two unrelated senses.

Examples of synesthesia:

- "The eye of man hath not heard, the ear of man hath not seen, man's hand is not able to taste, his tongue to conceive, nor his heart to report what my dream was." — William Shakespeare
- "Thy voice was a censer that scattered strange perfumes, and when I looked on thee I heard a strange music." — Oscar Wilde
- "Back to the region where the sun is silent." — Dante

What is prosody?

Prosody is the study of the tune and rhythm of speech and how these features contribute to meaning.

Prosody is the study of those aspects of speech that typically apply to a level above that of the individual phoneme and very often to sequences of words (in prosodic phrases). Features above the level of the phoneme (or "segment") are referred to as suprasegmentals. A phonetic study of prosody is a study of the suprasegmental features of speech.

At the phonetic level, prosody is characterised by:-

- vocal pitch (fundamental frequency)
- loudness (acoustic intensity)

- rhythm (phoneme and syllable duration)

Prosody Definition

Prosody (PROHZ-o-dee) is a method for studying metrical structures, particularly rhythmic and intonational patterns, of words. Prosody is generally discussed in the context of poetry, although it is also utilized, to a lesser extent, in prose.

The word derives from the Latin *prosodia*, meaning "accent of a syllable." The Latin meaning originated from the Greek *prosoidia*, which means both "song sung to music" and "accent modulation." The originating Greek word is formed from *pros*, meaning "to, near, forward," combined with *oide*, which means "song" or "poem." Prosody's first usage in English was in the late 15th century, when it was used to indicate "the study of versification."

Phonetic studies of prosody often concentrate on measuring these characteristics.

Prosody has been studied from numerous perspectives by people belonging to differing linguistic schools. There has been great diversity of approaches to prosody. Different approaches examine prosody from the perspective of grammar, of discourse, of pragmatics and of phonetics and phonology

Prosody can be regarded as part of the grammar of a language. Discourse approaches examine the prosody of normal interactions rather than stylised, constructed, fluent, scripted interactions. Functionalist approaches integrate the study of prosody with the study of grammar and meaning in natural social interactions.

Pragmatics examines the distinction between the literal meaning of a sentence and the meaning intended by the speaker. Prosody can have the effect of changing the meaning of a sentence by indicating a speaker's attitude to what is being said (eg. it can indicate irony, sarcasm, etc.) particularly when prosody works in conjunction with the social/situational context of an utterance.

Prosody overlaps with emotion in speech. The same acoustic features that are used to express prosody (intensity, vocal pitch, rhythm, rate of utterance) are also affected by emotion in the voice. For example, I can simultaneously be sad and ironic or fearful and sarcastic.

Speech contains various levels of information that can be described as:-

- Linguistic - direct expression of meaning
- Paralinguistic - may indicate attitude or membership of a speech community
- Non-linguistic - may indicate something about a speaker's vocal physiology, state of health or emotional state

Paralinguistic aspects of speech are those aspects that are not strictly linguistic, but which contribute to the meaning of an utterance. Paralinguistic features may help to indicate a speaker's attitude, although this may overlap with emotional aspects of speech.

Another paralinguistic aspect of speech are those features that indicate a speakers membership of a speech community. These are effectively sociolinguistic markers of speaker identity. eg. Australian versus New Zealand pronunciations, styles of speech of farmers versus bankers, etc.

Some speech communities might prefer broader pronunciations. Some speech communities might prefer more nasal voices. Some speech communities might speak louder or faster.

Gender has both paralinguistic and non-linguistic aspects. Some features may be regarded as more masculine or feminine by a particular speech community (eg. degree of pharyngealisation in Arabic)

But, features that are purely a consequence of physiological differences are non-linguistic aspects of speech

A speaker's emotional state is often evident in the speaker's voice. These features are linguistic to the extent that they are relevant to the meaning of the current utterance. On the other hand, our current emotional state might be a non-linguistic undertone to what is being said (ie. if its not very relevant to what's being said).

Our state of health can be evident in our speech. This would be a non-linguistic aspect of our speech. Note, however, that even this distinction can blur when the health issue is cognitive and affects the expression of meaning.

Segmental and suprasegmental features of speech are both affected by linguistic, paralinguistic and non-linguistic forces.

The main acoustic correlates of prosody (rhythm, intensity and fundamental frequency) are also correlates of paralinguistic and non-linguistic phenomena, particularly emotion.

Different Types of Prosody

There are four specific prosodic metrical patterns used for analyzing verse.

Syllabic Prosody

This style of analysis focuses on a fixed number of syllables in each line, independent of the stressed or unstressed emphasis. Syllabic prosody is particularly useful when studying poetic forms like the Japanese haiku or tanka.

Accentual Prosody

Unlike syllabic prosody, accentual prosody does not measure the number of syllables per line. It counts the number of stresses or accents each line contains. This type of prosody is particularly relevant for Germanic or Old English poetry.

Accentual-Syllabic Prosody

This type of prosody measures both the number of syllables and the patterns of emphasis in each line of verse. It is very commonly used in the analysis of English poetry and theatrical verse.

Quantitative Prosody

Rather than counting the number of syllables or stresses per line, quantitative prosody is concerned with the length (duration) or shortness of the syllables' pronunciation. This type of prosody is most relevant for studying classical Greek and Roman poetry; it very rarely applies to English poetry.

Prosody as a Linguistic Technique

While prosody is commonly considered a method for analyzing verse, it also is an important phonetics term. In linguistics, prosody is used to analyze suprasegmentals—elements of speech larger than the individual segments of consonants and vowels. This means that, in addition to syllables, linguistic prosody concerns itself with tone, stress, rhythm, intonation, and chunking (the perception of word groups or chunks based on pausing).

Linguistic prosody can also be used to analyze a speaker, including their emotional state and what they're saying. When analyzing speech, linguistic prosody often focuses on whether <u>irony</u> or <u>sarcasm</u> is intended; where emphasis is placed; whether what is spoken is intended as a statement, a command, or a question; and other elements of language not indicated by diction or syntax.

Finally, linguistic prosody distinguishes between auditory variables—subjective impressions experienced by the listener—and acoustic variables—the objectively measurable properties of sound waves. Auditory variables include the pitch of a voice, sound length, loudness or softness, and timbre (sound quality). Rhythm, tempo, and pausing are also important elements of linguistic prosody.

What is a syllable in English?

A syllable is a unit of spoken language that forms an entire word or parts of words. Syllables are usually made up of a single vowel sound and any surrounding consonant sounds. For instance, the word 'butter' contains two syllables: 'but' and 'ter'.

What Is Meter in Poetry?

Meter is the basic rhythmic structure of a line within a work of poetry. Meter consists of two components:

1. The number of syllables

2. A pattern of emphasis on those syllables

A line of poetry can be broken into "feet," which are individual units within a line of poetry. A foot of poetry has a specific number of syllables and a specific pattern of emphasis.

Common Types of Feet in Poetry

In English poetry, the most common types of metrical feet are two syllables and three syllables long. They're characterized by their particular combination of stressed syllables and unstressed syllables. They include:

Trochee. Pronounced DUH-duh, as in "ladder."

Iamb. Pronounced duh-DUH, as in "indeed."

Spondee. Pronounced DUH-DUH, as in "TV."

Dactyl. Pronounced DUH-duh-duh, as in "certainly."

Anapest. Pronounced duh-duh-DUH, as in "what the heck!" (Anapestic poetry typically divides its stressed syllables across multiple words.)

Common Types of Meter in Poetry

Metrical feet are repeated over the course of a line of poetry to create poetic meter. We describe the length of a poetic meter by using Greek suffixes:

one foot = monometer

two feet = dimeter

three feet = trimeter

four feet = tetrameter

five feet = pentameter

six feet = hexameter

seven feet = heptameter

eight feet = octameter

Examples of Meter in Poetry

When you combine the stress patterns of specific poetic feet with specific lengths, you unlock the many possibilities of poetic meter. A good example of this is "iambic pentameter," which can be found in English language poetry across many centuries.

Iambic pentameter contains five iambs per line, for a total of ten syllables per line. Every even-numbered syllable is stressed. William Shakespeare is the most famous practitioner of iambic pentameter in the English literary canon. Each of Shakespeare's 154 sonnets features rhyming iambic pentameter—specifically adhering to an ABAB CDCD EFEF GG pattern. This is exemplified by "Sonnet 114":

Types of Metrical Feet

So far, students have heard, performed, compared, and created syllable patterns. But they haven't named them. It's time to name them. In general, the combinations of syllables are called metrical feet. And it probably won't surprise you that each foot—stressed/unstressed, unstressed/stressed, etc—has a name. There are four types of feet that poets most commonly use.

Trochee: a trochee (pronounced TROH-kee) occurs when two syllables follow the pattern stressed/unstressed. In other words, the stress happens on the FIRST of two syllables (as in table and birthday.)

Iamb: an iamb (pronounced EYE-amb) occurs when two syllables follow the pattern unstressed/stressed. In other words, the stress happens on the SECOND of two syllables (as in because and surprise.)

Notice that these two metrical feet, the trochee and the iamb, are duple-ish. The next two are triple-ish.

Dactyl: a dactyl (pronounced DAK-til) occurs when three syllables follow the pattern stressed/unstressed/ unstressed. In other words, the stress happens on the FIRST of three syllables (as in sharpener and totally.)

Anapest: an anapest (pronounced AN-i-pest) occurs when three syllables follow the pattern unstressed/ unstressed/stressed. In other words, the stress happens on the LAST of three syllables (as in interrupt, clarinet, unprepared).

There is such a thing as an amphibrach (AM-fi-brak), which is a syllable pattern of unstressed/stressed/ unstressed, but only linguists care about it; poets don't.

Here are three more words students need to know:

Spondee: a spondee occurs when two syllables follow the pattern stressed/stressed. In other words, two adjacent syllables have the same stress. Here's an example from a famous speech about the Berlin Wall given by Ronald Reagan. Reagan said, "Tear down this wall!" In this sentence, the syllables tear and down make up a spondee because they are stressed equally. Here's another example, this one from a Shakespeare Sonnet: Rough winds do shake the darling buds of May. Rough winds! The spondee makes the winds pretty rough indeed!

Catalexis (ca-ta- LEX-is): Doesn't it sound like a European sports car? Actually, a catalexis occurs when one or two syllables do not appear at the end of a line, even though you expect them to be there.

Example: Most of the words that I give you are new.

Let's examine this sentence. Most of these / words that I / give you are / new.

The words in between two slashes make up a foot of poetry. The foot that begins the line (Most of these) is a dactyl. Each foot should have three syllables with the first syllable stressed, because that's the way the line starts. But notice the way the line ends. "New" is a stressed syllable; but where are the two unstressed syllables that should follow it? THEY'RE NOT THERE! When a line ends with syllables that are missing, we say that the line ends with a catalexis (or a catalectic foot). Now, let's go on to the ...

Anacrusis (a-na-KROO-sis): This occurs when an extra syllable is placed at the beginning of a line, even though you don't expect the extra syllable to be there. It has basically the same meaning in poetry and music. The only difference I can see is that the anacrusis in poetry is a break in an expected pattern; an anacrusis in music is an upbeat pattern that (usually) does not violate our expectations. Hey, check out this rhymed couplet I made up.

Most of the / words that I / give you are / new.

You'll / use them in / poems be / fore we are / through.

The second line should begin with a stressed syllable because the first line began that way. But sometimes poets don't like to do that. In this case, the word that starts the second line—you'll—is unstressed. It's an extra syllable I just stuck in there before the first stressed syllable use. That extra syllable is called an anacrusis.

Also, did you notice something peculiar about the feet in the second line? /poems be/ is one foot. And /fore we are/ is another foot. In order to analyze the line—to scan it accurately—as a series of dactyls, we had to break up the word before into be- and -fore. My students didn't have to do that when we were hearing and performing metrical feet in isolation. A few pages ago we used intact words. But here's the interesting thing. If we heard the foot /poems be/ in isolation we would have no idea how it functions metrically. It's only when we place it in a series that the foot contributes to our understanding of the meter of the line. It's the same in music. One pattern by itself tells us very little. A string or chain of patterns tells us much more.

****

www.ingramcontent.com/pod-product-compliance
Lightning Source LLC
Chambersburg PA
CBHW040757120726
48005CB00012B/1206